THE EYES HAVE IT

THE EYES HAVE IT

(Wanderings Part 2)

JOHN E. BEERBOWER

P.J.Bear

CONTENTS

**To my daughter Sarah,
my pupil and my teacher**

"The curate was wandering,
but the liberty of wandering was essential
to his talking with the kind of freedom and truth
he wanted to mediate
betwixt his pupil and the lovely things he saw."

George McDonald
Thomas Wingfold, Curate
(1880)

Preamble

Typing with all ten,
while my fingers could.
Dictating to a computer,
while my voice held.
Then, pecking away,
two fingers still worked.

Now, it is just the eyes.
So,
let the eyes have at it.

These essays are by necessity shorter than and without as many references as my prior collection. I hope that they are not too terse to be interesting. Compromises to reality had to be made.

But, it is difficult to stop.

JUST ME

Chicken or What?

AVOIDANCE

I have already written at some length, and more or less contemporaneously, about my coping methods in the early days. These reflections are made with hindsight.

For the first five years, I semi-consciously avoided information about people with ALS. I preferred not to know anything beyond my own experience. Very early, still in England, I had visited a respiratory clinic for people with the disease. We were separated just by curtains. Arrivals were staggered, so I did not see any of the others, but I could hear. I could hear the woman on my right struggle to speak. I could hear the woman on my left describe her husband's troubles over the prior months, her troubles. As soon as I was done, I rushed out, back to my car.

At the George Washington Hospital clinic, it was easier. We had staggered arrivals and private consultation rooms. And, I always left early. I did not wait for the mental health folks to ask if I was having thoughts of suicide. The first time, they got all agitated when I responded "Not today." I was joking. But, I thereafter avoided them. I stick with people who laugh at my jokes.

Over the past two years, I have taken some interest in others with this affliction.

I was shocked by stories about people who continued to travel. What was wrong with me? Were we being too cautious? I could not imagine how I would board an airplane, get down the aisle, get into my seat. I use a lift for all transfers. I sit in a power wheelchair that weighs 450 pounds. I am quite uncomfortable in any other chairs. Even recliners can not make the necessary adjustments.

However, assuming I could board directly from the gate and have my wheelchair safely transported, I would still have to be transferred by lift into the transfer chair to board and again by lift into my seat. But, the lift cannot move me sideways into the seat, only forwards and backwards. It would take two or three men to lift and carry me by hand. The same situation at the destination. I checked chartering a plane. I can not legally fly in my wheelchair, so the same issues apply, plus the additional problem of getting me up the stairs to the door. The same with dressing. I marvel at how dressed up some ALS sufferers are. Again, they may be able to stand or be much smaller. The TV crime shows stress how hard it is to dress a dead body. I can confirm that that is also the case for a live body that cannot help.

So, these more adventurous people must either still be able to stand or not be 6'3" and over 200 pounds.

Am I just more cautious than others, more of a chicken?

THEN MORE

I have been regularly quite surprised by how resilient, stubborn and active many sufferers of ALS seem to be. It is almost puzzling. But, unlike other fatal diseases, the increasing incapacitation comes from muscle weakness, not from pain. Thus, the real challenges are emotional and psychological. Immense but surmountable.

"[S]easons of suffering have a way of exposing the deepest parts of ourselves and reminding us that we're not the people we thought we were. People in the valley have been broken open. They have been reminded that they are not just the parts of themselves that they put on display. There is another layer to them they have been neglecting, a substrate where the dark wounds, and most powerful yearnings live. Some shrivel in the face of this kind of suffering. They seem to get more afraid and more resentful. They shrink away from their inner depths in fear. Their lives become smaller and lonelier. ... But for others, this valley is the making of them. The season of suffering interrupts the superficial flow of everyday life. They see deeper into themselves and realize that down in the substrate, flowing from all the tender places, there is a fundamental ability to care, a yearning to transcend the self and care for others. ...Their life is defined by how they react to their moment of greatest adversity."

David Brooks, *The Second Mountain* (2019), pp.xii-xiii.

My daughter was sharing with me this morning her thoughts stimulated by a podcast from a woman dying of cancer. I must steal some of her observations. My daughter says:

"We always say how lucky people are who die unexpectedly in their sleep, but maybe they miss something, something important. As the body crumbles around you, so often do parts of the emotional and psychological baggage one is carrying—jealousies, resentments, defensiveness, even some fears. In the process, the 'spirit' [my word; I suspect she would prefer to say 'something mysterious and unknowable'] starts to grow, to expand."

Yes. A chance, in the words sung by Tim McGraw, "to live like you are dying." But, not with sky diving or bull riding or mountain hiking. No "bucket lists". The hard way. Indeed, the song does not do justice to the potential inner experience. There is an opportunity to achieve a peace, a feeling of acceptance and a mindfulness that elude most healthy, active people.

"Sometimes you experience your first taste of nobility in the way you respond to suffering. ...The right thing to do when you are in moments of suffering is to stand erect in the suffering. Wait. See what it has to teach you. Understand that your suffering is a task that, if handled correctly, with the help of others, will lead to enlargement, not diminishment."

David Brooks, *The Second Mountain,* pp.36, 38.

The years following my diagnosis were the truly transformative. I wrote about them in *Wanderings of a Captive Mind.* But, "I will say I did not come out of that pit with empty hands. Life had to beat me up a bit before I was tender enough to be touched. It had to break me a bit before I could be broken open. Suffering opened up the deepest sources of the self and exposed fresh soil for new growth." David Brooks, *The Second Mountain,* p.230.

AND, NOW

Of course, there are also those sufferers who just quit, who resign themselves (and their families and friends) to a quicker but joyless end. "Some shrivel in the face of this kind of suffering. They seem to get more afraid and more resentful. They shrink away from their inner depths in fear. Their lives become smaller and lonelier." *Id.,* p.xiii. There is not much to say to or about them.

I also feel badly listening to and reading the comments of those sufferers who appear to be obsessed with the prospect of a cure. One will come, maybe in time for some of these people. But, will it be just preventative? I think it will be a long time before we have a treatment that can reverse the effects. Meanwhile, these people are depriving themselves and their families of a rare opportunity.

Sad.

I Miss My Tooth, Sometimes

The inescapable human dilemma—the present versus the future. Whether to consume now at the expense of the future or to save for it. And, the related dilemma, perhaps for the more philosophically inclined, quality versus quantity.

I

About a year ago, I suddenly lost an inlay and part of the remaining tooth. It was the last molar on the top left, known to dentists as Tooth 16. A brief visit to the dentist indicated that the repair would entail pretty extensive work, which would be challenging for someone confined to a wheelchair and dependent on a ventilator to breathe. After brief deliberations, we concluded that the best course would be to have what was left of the tooth removed. The procedure should only take 10 minutes, and what would I need with the molar, anyway, if I would not be chewing much.

Everyone forgot about my impacted wisdom teeth.

In the event, the extraction required three sessions of over 10 minutes each, between which the oral surgeon disappeared (presumably to vent his frustrations). I faired pretty well, with my daughter monitoring my oxygen continuously and the dental assistant demonstrating impressive proficiency with the suction. Of course, we can not know if an inlay or crown would have been as manageable.

I am coping fine, but sometimes I miss my tooth.

II

Early on, the clinic recommended that I have a feeding tube inserted so as to have it when I needed it. They wanted to do it while my breathing was still good to minimize the risk that I would be unable to breathe on my own following the sedative. (I later discovered that they meant after the procedure, not during.) So, I did it. Not so bad, but followed by a truly miserable night in the hospital for observation. I was fine for months until the tube fell out one night. Off to the ER. Parking is easy after 1:00 am. The replacement fell out too, in the shower. I had two more before I started using it for food. By then, I could no longer breathe on my own anyway.

III

A similar, but more consequential decision is to trach or not. The doctors say that it is better to have a scheduled tracheostomy rather than an emergency one. They also prefer that it be done while you are still relatively strong and healthy. I certainly understand the doctors' preferences.

But, for the patient, the procedure effectively means no more talking and no more eating or drinking. For someone in my condition, the trach will be irreversible. Of course, there is also the risk of the procedure and the hospital stay and period of recovery, a matter now made much more serious by the dire shortage of registered nurses for home trach care. I might never get home again.

On the plus side, it would no longer be necessary to wear the mask, with the attendant sore and itchy spots on my face and head, so I should be more comfortable and my face will be visible. The doctors think that after a trach, it will be easier for people to suction congestion from my lungs, but I have doubts. Now, we use the cough assist machine to break up the congestion and help pull up the secretions, and I can participate, both physically and by determining what is needed. I have trouble imagining how the nurse would be able to accomplish the same thing. Yet, at some point, the cough assist and external ventilator may prove inadequate, whereas the ventilator with the trach might suffice. Might. For a while.

One year ago, I had a consultation with a surgeon. At that point, I was speaking reasonably well (I could generally be understood), and I was still eating many things. Now, however, I can barely communicate by voice, and most of my nutrition comes through the tube. Yet, I still drink coffee a couple of times a day and wine every evening. And, I can eat things that melt in my mouth, like dark chocolate and soft cheeses. So, the sacrifice would still be significant.

I assume that the benefits are the likelihood of a longer life and of a less traumatic death. The first is not important to me; the second matters a lot, because of the potential impact on my care-givers.

So?

No answer yet. Delaying the decision may make it for me, in various different scenarios (poor health, death, so on). But, I still have a little over a case of very good wine and some 60 year old cognac. So, the time is not right.

What lessons can we find here?

Only that the pervasive uncertainty we face makes agonizing over the supposed choices and decisions rather pointless and silly. We do not really face these dilemmas, only the illusion of them. We stumble forward, doing our best. But, I do take exception to the frequent advice: "Live for today." Instead of "live for today," one should just be sure to "live today" and be ready for tomorrow.

Who Am I?

"Then something ... woke up inside him,
and he wished to go and see the great mountains,
and hear the pine-trees and the waterfalls,
and explore the caves,
and wear a sword instead of a walking-stick."

J.R.R. Tolkien
The Hobbit

I start at the beginning.

My father grew up on a small farm in a very small town in Northwestern Ohio, appropriately called Hicksville. Its claim to fame is that it is mentioned in *Huckleberry Finn*. My mother's father during the 1930s worked at the YMCA so that his family could eat meals in the cafeteria. That was his pay. My parents both graduated from Ohio State. They married right after my father returned from Italy, where he had served in the army. I grew up in southern Michigan, where everyone was either management or labor and supported either Michigan or Ohio State (in football). Our town was economically diverse, but otherwise pretty homogeneous. Our minority were Catholics. My father was quite successful over time. We moved to Oakwood, a suburb of Dayton, Ohio, which was much less economically diverse (but there were more different religions). My parents lived quite well after all four kids were through college and had several wonderful years of travel and adventure after he retired.

THE CHILD

I always felt like an outsider looking in, just a voyeur. From as far back as I can remember. Maybe 4 or 5. Like the baby that just sits and stares. Watching everyone. Feeling invisible. I have continued to be a person who stares, who observes. (Of course, now it is about all I can do. But, why before?)

When I was about 5, my brother and I were playing in our sandbox with a girl of my age who lived down the street. I did not notice that she noticed I was staring. She kicked sand in my eyes. I was crying while my mother washed it out, but I was mainly embarrassed, fearing that she would conclude (realize) that I liked her. The day was saved when my brother tried to retrieve a toy soldier and got his arm stuck in a steel pipe sticking up from the ground. My mother poured vegetable oil on his arm and called the fire department. By the time the firemen arrived, the oil had done its work. His arm slipped right out when the fireman pulled.

Around this age, I would have dreams that I could fly, watching people from above, or that I could make myself invisible. Actually, I think that they were daydreams or fantasies that were played in my mind as I was trying to go to sleep at night. At this time, I also acquired the practice of climbing up into an enormous weeping willow tree we had and hiding there to watch the world. I assumed (mistakenly) that no one could see me. I do not know if these fantasies were common or unusual. In fact, something I wondered about during my childhood was the extent other kids were the same as I was, what they thought about, what they did when alone.

A few years later, now living in Northville, I went to summer camp for a week on a large lake in Michigan. One night, we were joking around, teasing each other. I made some comment involving hair and either teeth or a toothbrush. The cabin counselor jumped all over me. I was scared but particularly upset because I had no idea what I had done. It haunted me. Many years later, I concluded that he must have thought I had made a joke about oral sex! I was not that precocious. But, as a result of this incident, I have always been a little concerned about my comprehension of social interactions.

One day, a little later, I was outside for recess, off by myself trying to look occupied. It was a cold day and I had my hands in my coat pockets. I had started a slow trot across the playground, when a ball from a dodge ball game bounced off the wall and rolled toward me. I did not see it in time and stepped right on it. Next thing I remember was being led down the school's hallway trying to catch the blood dripping from my face in my cupped hands. I learned the benefits of hydrogen peroxide, however. My face was carefully cleaned and healed quickly. The scrap on my right wrist was overlooked by the nurse in the excitement and took forever to heal.

In hindsight, I think my biggest fear in childhood was of being embarrassed. Especially of being embarrassed in person, to my face, so to speak. It was not rejection or losing that frightened me so much. It was the prospect of public humiliation, of being made fun of. Again, I am not sure why. Maybe because my family found undue amusement in the teasing of one another. Maybe because of a fundamental lack of self confidence. I also was very nervous about the possible embarrassment of others. Because I would be very embarrassed to cause someone else's embarrassment.

In any event, it made me quite reserved; sometimes, I think people thought I was shy, but really I was intimidated or just scared. Actually, I usually handled my own embarrassment pretty well when it happened.

But, I was still afraid. (My current affliction certainly cured that; I cannot imagine what could embarrass me now.) Despite all of this, I apparently projected something that was often interpreted as strength. In September 2021, I was reminiscing with one of my best friends from 60 years ago, with whom I had lost contact for decades. He wrote:

> "I have a vivid memory of the time when you led a bunch of 3rd graders to attack and overwhelm a bully 6th grader on the playground. ... I was not a participant in or an observer of this incident because I was one of those students who went home for lunch... I always felt left out from not having participated in this legendary event. Did this really happen or am I imagining heroics that I wished were real?"
>
> Just his fantasy

(I think!)

THE YOUTH

We lived a comfortable, but certainly not extravagant, life. I never had my own room or a 10 speed bike or a leather jacket. I did not have a car in college. I did not travel abroad until after I finished law school. Family vacations had generally been by car, staying at motels, breakfasts of donuts and juice. I loved it. From 13 onward, I worked every summers but one when I attended a National Science Foundation math program at Oregon State University.

I was always obsessed with projects. I could not stand doing nothing. Model ships and airplanes. Arts and crafts. Gardening. I painted lead soldiers, baskets for handbags, posters, and more. Reading was a big part of my youth. (The pursuit of hobbies continued through adulthood. In my 50s, I still could not let a large snowfall pass without building an igloo, a fort or snow sculptures. In retirement, I started writing and tried to return to the piano, painting and some serious bike riding. But, I encountered some significant physical problems, presumably my first symptoms.)

I was not physically brave, certainly not reckless or daring. I tried to avoid getting hurt. At the same time, I have always had a pretty high tolerance for pain, at least by New York City standards. I guess I could take it, but I would not invite it and would shudder to see it coming. Also, I was tall, with broad shoulders and better than average athletic ability (only slightly better).

Twice, I had a teacher call me an "enigma": once at 13 and again at 20. The confrontation with my seventh grade teacher was a bit heated, on her part. I think I said nothing. My college political science professor was more contemplative about the situation. I was equally mute. Both clearly were disappointed in me. Unrealized potential, I guess. A non-participant in class and generally unemotional and passive. I was always a strong student in my written work and with exams, though, and was well liked by most of my teachers and most mothers.

Pretty early I developed sort of a martyrdom obsession. I went to the musical Camelot, then later read T. H. White's *The Once and Future King*. I identified with Wart, as Arthur is called in the book. I loved the movie *Becket*, with inspired performances by Peter O'Toole and Richard Burton. In college, I was very moved by Albert Schweitzer's *The Quest of the Historical Jesus* (He "lays hold of the wheel of the world to set it moving on that last revolution which is to bring all ordinary history to a close. It refuses to turn, and he throws himself on it. Then it does turn; and crushes him," pp.370-71). And, I was taken by Albert Camus ("It is during that return, that pause, ... I see that man going back down with a heavy yet measured step toward the torment of which he will never know the end. That ... is the hour of consciousness. At each of those moments when he leaves the heights and gradually sinks toward the lairs of the gods, he is superior to his fate. He is stronger than his rock," *The Myth of Sisyphus and Other Essays*).

A little later, I read the novels by John le Carré about George Smiley. As le Carré wrote in a 2000 Introduction to a reprint of *Smiley's People*, "Smiley was still my hero, but ... [h]is radicalism was the thinker's, not the doer's. Ultimately, whatever his misgivings, he always knuckled down and did the job, even if he had to leave his conscience outside the door."

Sacrificing, taking on the burdens of others, being a martyr. That seemed to be the basis of a meaningful life—"he ain't heavy, he's my brother." In my fantasy world, I seemed not to grasp the fact that for most martyrs, the glory comes after they are dead. I was also a sucker for anyone willing to ask for help. I wanted to take care of people, to be a guardian and a provider, like my father was. In the end, I did not do nearly as well as he did. (I still tell myself that I faced a much more difficult world than he did, but more than some of the difficulties clearly of my own making.)

In all of this, I gravely overestimated my own strength. Think, Walter Mitty runs face first into hard reality. All in all, I neglected myself and failed to recognize my own needs. In thinking about it, I now realize that I had become a made-to-order victim or, in today's parlance, an incurable "enabler".

It was not until my mid-40s that I read T. H. White's sequel, *The Book of Merlin*. There, Arthur, alone, late at night, in his tent, awaiting the final battle with Modred, knowing he would be defeated, all lost, all for naught. I found it the most depressing book I had ever read. The image haunted me. (The second most depressing was Cormac McCarthy's *The Road*, some two decades later. Was there a glimmer of hope in his last image of the trout in the clear, sparkling mountain stream? The third was William Manchester's *A World Lit Only By Fire*, which was in the 1980s. It upended my beliefs about human development and Christianity. Years later, I discovered that the Dark Ages were not nearly as dark and were much more nuanced than Manchester described.)

Something else happened while I was in college—I willed myself to be open minded. I actually remember the specific event. I put myself in the position of someone else, as a matter of logical reasoning, and asked what that me would want. The first example was a taste of feminism. I asked myself what educational and career opportunities would I want if I were a woman. Pretty lame, but a revelation for me. I applied that process to other situations. I did not suddenly become empathetic. I became intensely rational, committed to reason and reasoning. Cold and unfeeling, really. But, much less bigoted.

Curiously, the end result was the undermining of my confidence in my own opinions. I suffered a lapse into helpless relativism. That development reinforced my existing tendency to withdraw inward. I found myself resorting more and more to irony and sarcasm. Actually, mostly sarcasm. It was a good strategy for New York City. Oddly, most people did not notice. They were so engrossed in themselves, in what I was mocking, I guess.

THE ADULT

After my university endeavors, I went to New York City. I was pretty frightened much of the time at first. But, the months went by. I got used to the subway—very loud, dirty and with trains that looked like locomotives mistakenly running indoors. I learned to protect my wallet on the subway, to be relatively inconspicuous, to walk on the street side of the sidewalk, away from doorways and alleys. This was the City in the mid-1970s, after all, pre-Giuliani, when muggers were a bigger danger than out of control taxis. (Over 40 years, however, I knew more people killed by taxis than by muggers.)

I apparently projected a commanding presence with a severely judgmental demeanor. (In fact, I did not become judgmental until I was over 30. And, I do not even know why. I did not feel superior, but I knew I was when it came to work. And, it was about most people's basic incompetence that I was critical.) In truth, I did have a strong moral streak that people noticed and interpreted as judgmental or arrogant. I also suffered from an explosive temper, like my father. Maybe from denying my feelings any outlet. Also, like my father.

My work was consuming, and, in October 1980, six years (and some, 16,000 billable hours) later, I became a partner at the Firm. (By the way, an honest 10 billable hour day generally required 12-13 hours in the office.)

And, within a couple of years, I had become addicted to the City. Of course, the money helped. I was making $13,000 a month; but I was also mesmerized to be surrounded by so much talent and ability. I loved the abundance of culture and the level of knowledge and intellect in the City. The architecture, the art, the music, the dance and, even the fashion. The best of everything. I was never meant to be a big fish in any pond. I was always in the top 10%, never number one, regardless of the quality of the pool. It seems my performance rose to maintain my relative position as the quality of the competition increased. Thus, I felt a drive to put myself with and against the best. However, I still always felt on the fringe.

I disliked the people on the Upper Westside, so many over aged pretend intellectuals, with scraggly beards, long unkempt hair and sandals. Proclaimed liberals but ruthless in getting to the front of the line, in keeping rent-controlled housing, in securing free street parking. On the Upper Eastside I felt more comfortable, because of the veneer of gentility. Up close, I disliked many of the residents—social climbing, back biting, shallow, snobbish and often tasteless. But, at a distance... Well, I was more at ease with their appearance.

Nonetheless, there were some residents I really liked, hidden away, like secret gardens. People who were elegant and gracious, with surprising talents and interests. Occupying niches, quietly, in the big city.

I read constantly, alternating intense periods of fiction and non-fiction (mainly science for the lay person). I became a devoted runner (well, jogger), clocking 20-5 miles a week. I developed a strong interest in opera. Not surprisingly, I had no real friends.

In truth, I also had become something of a snob. I liked quality clothes, expensive shoes, decent wine, good food. I developed strong views as to what constituted good, and bad, taste. We generally stayed at Relais & Chateaux hotels when we traveled in Europe. And, so on. I had succumbed to temptation. And, I was to pay.

So,I finished my schooling with no debt of my own and only a modest debt of my wife, which we quickly paid off. I received no inheritance beyond $10,000 from my maternal grandfather when I was in my late 20s. I worked very hard, took some risks.

My side hobby/business was home renovation. In the beginning, I did a lot of the work myself, such as wallpapering and painting in the middle of the night. Later, I mostly did designs and fought with contractors. I actually derived considerable pleasure from these projects. Unlike the asymmetry of competitions or litigation, where the pain of losing is far greater than the joy of winning, the results of renovation projects bring feelings ranging from depression to glee. It is like one great learning experience. You could always start again (if the money lasted) and you could always do better. The thrill and satisfaction of creating and the deep happiness of creating beauty. What a combination. (Landscaping offered me the same.) And, I made money. (In New York in the 1980s, it was hard to lose in real estate.) Actually, I made enough money to end up in the top 0.1 %.

Big surprise.

NOW

Now that I am "immune" to embarrassment, I can "speak". I need not hide my opinions. I do not worry anymore about offending people (not so much anyway). I dealt with my prejudices through reason and reasoning. I "thought" myself to acceptance and tolerance, even though I did not much like people.

When reading *Wanderings of a Captive Mind,* an old friend said: "Although I have to admit that your points of view do not fall comfortably into a 'PC compatible' category, I do not find them in the least 'offensive.' You have brought a fierce belief in rational argument to bear on subjects that are seldom considered appropriate to reasoned debate. At this point ... in my life, I do not share your faith in logical arguments." Actually, it is a fierce belief in the powerfulness of reasoning itself, for oneself, not for argument or persuasion. Driven by a need to understand, to see and to try to know, even though inevitably doomed to failure. That is what I had sought in writing *Important Things,* as well.

The set backs and challenges of the years have not dulled the keenness of that need.

My Career

In my law firm, I was also on the fringe. I guess I lacked the necessary team spirit. And, I was not skilled at office politics—garnering the credit while avoiding the blame, recognizing when to keep quiet, knowing when to look the other way. I was certainly not good at self-promotion.

However, I was sought out by certain non-ligation partners for matters that they thought were not suitable for the litigation department generally. As a result, I handled a large number of rather unusual cases as the sole partner. In the process, I probably argued more appeals and examined more witnesses than any of my partners over my 37 years of practice.

On the whole, my reputation was mixed. A corporate partner with whom I did merger and acquisitions work said to me very late one night that he was perplexed by me. Some people told him I was the best lawyer they had ever encountered, while some of my litigation partners said I was always making mistakes. I just listened, no comment.

I

In fact, both groups were wrong. I could do the work of two or three other lawyers. I wrote well and quickly. (That presented a challenge for our system. The associates did the first drafts and the partner revised and edited. This worked normally. For example, one of my partners was a brilliant editor but he could agonize for an hour writing a one page letter. It was also how associates were suppose to learn.) My analytical abilities were second to none, and I was innovative, creative and imaginative in fashioning arguments. To my great surprise, I even turned out to be good on my feet in the courtroom.

However, I lacked litigation instincts. I could not anticipated, and thereby prepare for, my opponents' tactics. I was not a strategic thinker. I did not focus on evidentiary issues and opportunities. And, I could be timid about making objections or other spur of the moment decisions that might be controversial or antagonize a judge. I did not trust my judgments without time to consider.

An example. In a particularly heated hearing, my very experienced and much older opponent, representing the plaintiff, made a tactical decision not to call as his witness my senior executive, planning to get what he needed on cross examination. (I had also listed the executive as my witness.) After my opponent rested, I realized that if I rested my case after putting on just my expert witness, the plaintiff probably would not have carried its burden of proof. I hesitated. Very nervous. The judge had shown sympathy with the plaintiff previously; I was the out-of-towner, on the home turf of both the plaintiff and his lawyers. I did not want to appear too slick or clever. I certainly did not want to anger the judge. I was saved by the judge himself. He summoned me to the bench and asked me how long my remaining case would take. I took a deep breath and said that I was inclined to rest. "Up to you." So I did. There were howls of outrage from plaintiff's counsel, all three of whom rushed the bench, demanding to be allowed to reopen their case. The judge looked at me and said, "Well, Mr. Beerbower, do you agree?" I said, "No, your Honor." "The hearing is over," he ruled. (We won.)

It did not turn out so well all the time. I was yelled at by judges pretty often. In one case, the judge's courtroom clerk said, "Don't worry. It is because you remind her of her ex-husband." Great. My poor client!

Another time, while arguing an appeal before a three judge panel of the Eighth Circuit, one judge asked me why we had not offered to settle. I responded, "We did." One of the other two judges angrily rebuked me, saying that I had half an hour to find evidence of that fact in the appellate record. To my relief (and surprise), my associate did so. (We won.)

(In contrast, before a panel of the Sixth Circuit, my opponent was unable to answer some questions about the context of the dispute. I was asked whether I could explain what was really going on. I hesitated, took a deep breath, and then did so, favorably to my client. I then held my breath. The judge in the center leaned back in his chair and, in a stage whisper, said to his colleagues, "Finally, someone who knows the facts." (We won.) For the non-lawyers, appellate judges often form views of a case before oral argument and seek to elicit support for their views from the advocates.)

II

Judges can be very dignified and civil; they can also be pretty mean.

When the Amtrak Metroliner broke down in the middle of New Jersey causing me to miss an oral argument, the Chief Judge of the Third Circuit demanded to see my ticket to ascertain whether I had taken a prudently early train. (I had.)

In one case, we were docketed number 4 on a motion day. I decided we could arrive a few minutes later than usual, as a result. When we quietly entered the courtroom, I realized that the judge was waiting for me, with almost 50 lawyers in the audience waiting their turn. As I scrambled to the counsel table, the judge announced to the room, "Mr. Beerbower. You were always on time when you were winning." He proceeded to rebuke me for papers I had just filed, with the largest audience possible. To my amazement, as I left, two lawyers stood up and shook my hand, expressing their sympathy. And, they did so right in front of the judge. Apparently, he was known for such behavior and not well liked.

III

And, my abilities did not go unnoticed.

After the (successful) end of a criminal case in which we had represented the corporation and very experienced criminal counsel from the area represented the individual defendants, one of those lawyers (who looked like Robert Duvall did at the time) came to visit me. He had a business proposition. He wanted me as his co-counsel to handle the motions and brief-writing, while he would deal with the clients and the jury work. He was sure we would be in great demand. And, he said, "These are great clients; they never complain about the bills and pay promptly—every Friday, in cash." (And, if we lose?) Of course, I need not inform my partners (or the IRS). I passed, but I could not help wondering what I may have missed when watching the Netflix series *Ozark* 25 years later.

At the end of an arbitration in Mexico City, the arbitrators asked the CEO of the opposing party if he had anything else he would like to say. He responded, "Yes. Obviously, I had the wrong lawyer today."

One Federal judge described to his clerks my appearance on a major motion as "the perfect oral argument". Another experienced litigator called me "the best trial lawyer she had ever seen". Several times, I received widespread accolades for a cross-examination.

IV

The odd types of cases I handled resulted in many strange events. I had a fraud case as counsel to the plaintiff. We were trying to secure assets of the defendants. Tipped off that their yacht was being berthed at a local marina, I sent my associate to serve an order of attachment. When he arrived at the dock, a rather drunk older man greeted him saying, "If you're looking for the Lady (_____), she ain't never been here!"

In the same matter, I tried a case against the defendants in Virginia in order to seize some ocean front property. We were before an impressive Virginia state court judge (who belonged in the movies). I was eliciting testimony about how the proceeds of the fraud had been used. We had covered the purchase from Harry Winston, which was consummated in the backseat of a limousine in a highway rest stop in New Jersey so as to avoid New York sales tax, and I was starting on the details of an indulgent weekend in Las Vegas when a junior high class came into the courtroom to observe. His Honor summoned me to the bench. "Mr. Beerbower," he said, "Would you be so kind as to move to another topic? You can return to the prostitutes when the children have left." I did.

Once, a trial was delayed because opposing counsel was under house arrest for failing to file tax returns for several years. When he returned to court (wearing an ankle bracelet), he apologized, saying, "I had a severe case of procrastination!" It was a very acrimonious dispute between our clients and he, I, and the judge had numerous shouting matches; but, I still rather liked him. He kept going, he was not a quitter.

I represented the defendant in a suit brought by an investment partnership. The court was in downtown Trenton. The two representatives of the partnership arrived in a limousine with two very burly companions. Their bodyguards, I assumed. It was a pretty rough neighborhood in those days. The hearing went extremely well (for my side). When the plaintiff's representatives went out, they were roughly shoved into the back of the limousine by the two burly observers. I surmised that the "boss" was not happy that they lost. Fortunately, he seemed not to blame the lawyers.

By the way, New Jersey was the one jurisdiction in which I was sanctioned, for over-zealous representation of my client and defying the judge's wishes. I was still young then.

V

One of my last matters before retirement was to represent Her Majesty's Treasury in submitting an *amicus* (friend of the court) brief to the U. S. Supreme Court. To my great satisfaction, Justice Scalia quoted from my brief in his opinion for the majority.

Traumas to Remember

"There are moments that are
made up of too much stuff
for them to be lived
at the time they occur."

John le Carré
Tinker, Tailor, Soldier, Spy
p.394

I had little reaction when we went to the coroner to view the body. I guess I was still a bit numb, and it felt like it was a duty that had to be performed. My daughter had accompanied me on the trip from Cambridge to London and then to the coroner's office. The process was, I think, pretty much what I had been expecting. The only real surprise was how small she was. So much damage done, and yet so small. For me, the most traumatic events around the death of my wife, other than the telephone notification of the discovery of her body, were my first visit to our flat following her death and the subsequent inquest.

I.

On that first visit, I had to speak to the concierge, trying to console him, and then I encountered the big padlock that the police had placed on the front door the night she was discovered. I think that the police were done, but the executor of the estate insisted that I not access the flat without them present. They finally arrived with the key. Three people I had never met. We entered, with me under surveillance. I was overwhelmed by how dead my flat felt, and empty.

It was, of course, filled with stuff, and a lot stuff I had never seen before. In the foyer was a new suitcase, opened but not unpacked. I was later to conclude that it was for a trip she had taken to The Royal Crescent Hotel in the Bath the weekend just past (to meet some man I did not know). There were new purchases everywhere, some still in bags, some out but with the tags still attached, all unused, all unworn. The bathtub had been emptied but not cleaned. I got some supplies and started cleaning. The representatives of the estate began to inventory the items of value, exclaiming over special discoveries. I had no idea what I was allowed to touch. The message light on the phone was blinking. Would anyone ever listen to the messages? (No.) I felt so alone. So isolated. So helpless.

To my great surprise, when we left, they did not replace the padlock. I was free to return to my flat. Thereafter, the executor appeared to begin to trust me. She was speechless when I turned over to her thousands of dollars worth of cash in various currencies which my daughter and I found around the flat. She seemed uncomfortable as I (truthfully) identified items of value that were my wife's, not joint property. I reported the items belonging to me that were missing, probably sold by my wife, so listed as stolen by the executor. I obviously did not understand the game. I provided the executor the information I had relevant to the estate. Because of a credit check on a dormant bank account, I had an unknown address in Palm Beach. Turned out my wife had an ocean front condominium in Florida. From a bill left on the desk, we discovered a full storage bin in a facility in London.

II.

The second traumatic event occurred three months later, the inquest. That was a completely new experience for me and one for which I was stunningly unprepared. I had been told that the life insurance company in the U.S.was sending someone to the hearing in London and that the payout to my children would be held up as a result. It was substantial, and I worried about what circumstances could jeopardize the coverage. I was nervous, because by then we had learned that my wife had made a new will six months before she died disinheriting our children, as well as me.

There was quite an audience. My daughter and I were given the autopsy report, and shortly thereafter the hearing started. The Examiner was very impressive. And, courteous. After each witness, she asked me if I had any questions. That was a surprise; I had expected just to watch. Suddenly, I felt like I was a party to the proceeding. But, what kind? What was my role, my interest? What should be my objectives?

The police witness was very circumspect and had nothing unexpected to say. The psychiatrist, however, was a shock. He was flip and cheerful. He clearly felt no responsibility. She had completely conned him (as she had all of the others). I felt that I had to demonstrate that he knew nothing about her, which I easily did. But, my questioning prompted the Examiner to ask me to testify. By the way, only when the Examiner showed the psychiatrist the results from the toxicology report did he became visibly upset and tried to disclaim any responsibility.

When we thought we were finished, an unfamiliar man in the gallery stood up and demanded to take the stand, claiming to be my wife's fiancee. He testified that they had become engaged and were debating where to live, since she had been offered a choice of certain ambassadorships by the President. He also testified that she been New York the week before at a hearing in the divorce court and was quite upset by my slick lawyerly tricks. As to those last claims, I had first hand knowledge. I had been at that hearing in New York, and she had not shown up. Her lawyer struggled to explain to the judge why she was not there and could not be reached by telephone. As to their relationship, I had no knowledge. During his rant, he also disclosed certain facts that the Examiner had chosen to leave out of the public record. How could he have known? Who was the source?

I was shell-shocked; dazed and completely unsettled. But, I had to go on. Numb, but still talking and walking. Thanks to the intruder, the *Daily Mail* found the story gossip-worthy; and by the time we boarded the train back to Cambridge, it was online and the next morning, out in print. My daughter suffered most from the publicity. I cannot figure out how I let myself get into such a mess. It was like a bad dream; actually, of the general sort I often have. My nightmares come true!

My daughter helped me sort through things in the flat. That is how we found the cash and about the weekend in Bath. We learned that she had recently hired a high-end matchmaking service for an obscene fee. Specializing in multi-millionaires. There was other information about her gentlemen friends. Not much about assets, however. We gradually answered some questions. The intruder did know my wife. Her camera had a couple of photos of the two of them together somewhere in the countryside. Presumably, a weekend away. Also, he had been in contact with my wife's sister following the death, and she had provided him all of the details he disclosed at the hearing. She is the only one we told. He also asserted a substantial claim against the estate for loans he claimed to have made to my wife, but he had no documentation and got nothing. As for the alleged engagement, all we really know was that she was frequently seeing other men during the several months prior to her death, and we found no mention of him in her papers.

After I read his final novel, *Silverview*, a Christmas present in 2021, I decided to reread the eight George Smiley novels by John le Carré. I was a bit puzzled by the first four, since the Smiley I remembered was barely there. Then I read the fifth. Ah. There was my George, as he realized fully that he had been betrayed by everything that mattered to him.

I first recognized my own betrayal in March of 2013. For the prior year, to the disapproval and disappointment of my daughter, I had committed myself to trying to salvage my marriage. We were largely in France. It was going okay, peaceful but distant. Then, one morning in France, I read some correspondence between her and a divorce lawyer. It was curious. She was then back in London briefly. Shortly thereafter, during a telephone call with her, I suddenly realized that it was all a setup. It had been an act, a charade. But, for 40 years? The visits to all of the psychiatrists, supposedly to find help, to reduce the problems, were really a form of self-indulgence and a means of stockpiling drugs for self medication. She did not want to change and never did. She liked what she was. And me? I was just a useful stooge, something to be manipulated and exploited. The correspondence I had seen was part of the planning. Had she intended me to find the papers? But, why?

Standing in the garden, the phone in my hand, my world collapsed. A cliché, I know, but I felt emptied, utterly hollow, utterly hollowed out. A bit cold, but with a feeling of clarity that I had never experienced before (and have not since). The sacrifices, the suffering, the strenuous efforts to understand, to be understanding, all simply feeding the disease. Virtually everything I had done to be giving, supportive, self-sacrificing was wrong. My actions were in good faith, I really believe, but were terribly misguided. I felt George Smiley, deeply. I left France, not to return utill after her death.

In mid-May 2013, I filed for divorce in New York and obtained an order to preserve the *status quo*. I was not actually trying to obtain a divorce, only a legal separation with an equitable distribution of assets. But, court assistance was necessary to obtain her 'cooperation".

Previously, I had bought, renovated and furnished a cooperative apartment in New York City. Foolishly, I had included her as joint owner. At that point, we had separate bank accounts (she had kept money she earned separate for years already). In mid-May, I returned from London, on my way to visit my mother in Ohio for her 89th birthday, to discover that my wife was in the process of having my paintings removed from the apartment to be sold (with the proceeds to her). I turned away the persons who came to appraise the furniture and remaining paintings. A court order seemed to be the only way to protect my property while I was not there.

So, I instructed my attorney to file. (I made the birthday dinner with my mother. Her last. She died later that year.)

In France, I had an account to pay the expenses, many by direct debit. She wanted to rent the main house. I agreed subject to the rent being deposited in that account to pay expenses, with the surplus to go to her periodically. In the event, she persuaded the rental agency to pay the rent to her, leaving me with the expenses. I had just mailed tax payments, which the agent knew, committing most of the rent payment due. I could not very well stop payment on cheques to the French government. I sought a court order to resolve the French matter, but she failed to appear at the hearing scheduled for late June 2014, and the matter was put over. Of course, the French issue was moot a month later (except for the rent payments she had taken, but I then had much bigger challenges with which to deal).

She found the fact of the proceedings very threatening, presumably because they would likely expose the truth. Ultimately, it turned out that she was also in the process of hiding assets abroad, discovered and recovered by the executor. She had sold or given away much of my personal property, never to be recovered.

As it happened, I consulted with a psychiatrist, a psychologist and a very experienced doctor of internal medicine during those last few years. Each told me there was no real likelihood of her improving, but each also assured me that our friends and neighbors would recognize what was happening. That reassurance helped me when she commenced public attacks against me. After she was gone, I discovered that the experts were completely wrong. She had fooled almost everyone. Our friends mostly took her side.

SEQUEL

The rest of the story is easy.

I prepared an eloquent and flattering obituary and had it published.

My minister said: "You were very gracious, but then I would not have expected less." I arranged for the cremation and then for her burial next to her mother in Pennsylvania. He wrote me: "Bless you for rising to the occasion to care for such details; it does not surprise me, however, as it is very true to who I have learned you to be—honorable to the end." Honorable? Not exactly what I felt like. But, sometimes you have no choice. Duty calls. So, I got to work trying to cleanup the messes.

I wish I could have expected less of myself.

Within a couple of months, I found out that I was very sick.

Such is life.

It was an unbelievable 24 months. Of course, through it all, my daughter stood beside, and suffered along with, me. Ironically, for her sacrifice, she has spent the subsequent 7 years keeping me alive and comfortable. As a further irony, her successful efforts in doing so have extended her burden by keeping me going. But, it all has created a powerful bond between us. And, for that bond and her invaluable assistance, I shall be eternally grateful.

SOCIETY and LIFE

Some Observations from the Chair

My view from the wheelchair is limited. Knees to shoulders, two people wide. But, I do notice things.

I

My principal caregivers are a wonderful team. When together in the morning, there is almost constant banter and teasing. I largely lay back, close my eyes and enjoy it. Occasionally, I join in. They always laugh at my jokes. Often, they debate the proper match of socks and shirt. The resulting atmosphere has been a great help as my mornings have become more challenging. The group cheerfulness is up-lifting. Nothing like a giggle!

I have had caregivers from at least 12 different countries over the five years. Many were quite reserved, but several talked a lot about the lives they lived, before and after coming to the States, about their childhoods, their family traditions, their religious views and practices. I learned a significant amount about the immigrant world and about people who immigrate. They often talk about discipline in their families when they were children and its importance. Some examples they agree were too extreme, but they seem not to doubt their fathers' good intentions. They also seem quite worried about today's youth—no "endurance," too soft, too indulged.

The people I have gotten to know made the journey themselves; they are not second or third generation Americans (like I had regularly encountered in school and work in my previous life). Interestingly, these relative newcomers tend to be less guarded, without pretense; they tend to be more open and candid. That does not necessarily make them more likeable, just different. I have found these individuals to be un- usually optimistic and positive, even in times of adversity. Again, these characteristics do not necessarily make them more likeable but do make them more likely to succeed. Of course, the ones I got to know were the ones who had made a commitment to speak English. They were the self-selected from a group that was already self-selected, the most moti- vated of people who had already demonstrated the willingness to take risks and the desire to improve their lives. Perhaps, I should not have been surprised.

I have also been very impressed with the Hispanics' sense of commu- nity and of community responsibility. It reminds me of my childhood in small town Michigan. No one suffers alone. The generosity toward their extended families is even greater, exceeding anything I had ever seen or experienced. It is unquestionably a wonderful thing for single parents. Every child has a family.

One amusing thing for me was the strict adherence to bottled water (of course, I understand the reason, which is not funny). But, we were recycling 50 or 60 half liter plastic bottles a week. One of my caregivers urged me to get a water filter. Although, I was quite happy with tap water, I bought the filter. Thereafter, my daughter and I drank filtered water, but all of my caregivers simply continued with bottled water, including the proponent of the filter. I declared that they would have to pick the water up themselves. I did not want my daughter to be carting home what grew to four 24 bottle cases each week. Then, Alexandria restricted what could be recycled, freeing up our blue bins.

I have observed unfortunately and to my distress that RNs, LPNs and even CNAs know almost nothing about home care; they cannot operate the equipment, do not appreciate the basic routines, do not understand the mechanics of the human body (or of anything else). They need extensive training.

Rather remarkably, my daughter effectively setup, and supervises a high-level training program for in home caregivers—best practices, practical tips, emergency procedures. People leave a job here knowing what they are doing (although, not everyone is trainable). It is an odd feeling to be gifting the community with competent care givers. It is an unintended service being performed for selfish reasons, but I hope some others will have more comfortable lives as a result.

III

I have a strong impression that the range of products for the handicapped has dramatically increased over the past six years. It may be mainly the result of my increased awareness.

For example, I did not realize that there were wheelchair accessible vehicles available for private use until my daughter watched a movie in which the handicapped protagonist was chauffeured around in a modified minivan by his love interest. Shortly thereafter, I began to investigate what was available. I bought a used Toyota where I could enter using a built-in ramp and could sit where the passenger front bucket seat would normally be. I now have a Ram ProMaster with a Braunability lift—a lot more room. Yet, I think that many more options exist today. Maybe, it is that I became acclimated to the high prices and have been willing to contemplate more options.

However, I am sure that there are now available a greater variety and higher quality wheelchair ramps than there were 5 years ago. The same for scooters and wheelchairs. There are wheelchairs with balloon wheels for use on the beach and wheelchairs with tank treads for rough terrain and wheelchairs with "floating" seats for steep inclines, keeping the rider upright while the base tilts. I think that there are more options for bathing or showering. More types of stationary lifts and home elevators. And, swimming pool lifts. Some of the more innovative and aesthetically pleasing designs are European and not easily obtained or serviced here.

The problem is keeping up to date and even knowing what to look for. There is a business opportunity here. Or, an opportunity for a meaningful public service.

IV

On the use of beards to deal with a double chin, there seems to be two schools of thought.

One believes that a beard can draw attention away from the double chin. Such people cultivate tidy, well groomed beards that follow the jawline. The double chin is left naked, but it is supposed that the onlooker's eye will be drawn to the handsome beard. It is to this school that I subscribe. It is also the right approach for a weak chin. The other school favors letting the beard grow on the neck as well, covering the double chin with hair. The assumption, I suppose, is that the beard creates an ambiguity as to what is hair and what is fat. Personally, I think this approach just makes the double chin more prominent. But, clearly several opera tenors think otherwise, as must their assistants (or they are just afraid to speak up). Of course, one can always let the beard grow so long that it completely hides the double chin and neck. But, that approach takes years and presents some hygiene issues.

Pet[ty] Peeves

Accidents happen. I have had many, some quite funny, but all pretty dangerous.

It reminds me of a teenager learning to drive a car—mistakes are essential to the learning process; you just hope and pray that everyone lives to laugh about them. When I started using the power wheelchair, I had some ramps installed so I could get outside. One of the longer ramps went down a drop of three steps. Trying it out, I drove right off the edge, tumbling with the 450 pound machine into some very large and full boxwood bushes. My two adult children had quite a time extracting me and my chair. I immediately ordered a ramp with side rails. There are many other examples.

But, what I am writing about here are not the life-threatening occurrences, but truly petty things—things of the sort one obsesses over when confined to a wheelchair or a bed unable to move.

- Even though I am pretty much unable to speak, everyone asks me "or" questions. Up or down? Now or later? Here or there? Mask or glasses? Compound questions that cannot be answered with a nod of the head. I frantically try to time my nods to the relevant phrases of the question. A quick "yes" immediately followed by a "no" and *vice versa*. About half the time the questioner draws the correct conclusion. About the same odds I would have if I just did not answer or they just did not ask.

- Curiously, it appears that when a yes-or-no question is asked, the questioner has generally already assumed the answer, so it does not matter what I respond. Again, the same odds, about 50/50, of obtaining the correct result.
- Some other people, however, feel compelled when asking or telling me something to step close, lean over and position their face just 3 or 4 inches from my nose. Not only is that very uncomfortable for me, but they are too close to observe my responses—hand signals, head movement, facial expressions.
- I get cold easily. So, I ask for a blanket. Just as I start to feel better, the caregiver decides to rearrange it, letting the cold air in. I grit my teeth. The second time, I groan. The third, I want to scream, but I cannot do so.
- Another thing. When lifting a cup or glass for me to drink, some insist on wrapping both hands around the cup or glass so all I see coming toward me are fingers and thumbs and elbows. Difficult for me to anticipate the contact and a hard way to enjoy coffee or wine.
- Or, loud or strange noises behind me without warning. (I cannot see behind without turning the whole chair).
- Or, whispering to me or to each other.
- One of the most exhausting thing is people stepping right in front of my wheelchair just as I start to move. (Same with my daughter's dogs.) I have an excessive fear of running over someone's toes or paws. Our combined weight is over 650 pounds, and I cannot see the ground around my wheels. As a result, I over react. And, such quick movements are very taxing for me.

Grievances?

No. But, petty annoying.

Olive Oil

From 2006-21, we owned a property in France, between Cannes and Grasse. It was called Mas du Riou, on Chemin des Jasmins in the commune .of Chateauneuf de Grasse.

The main stone house (the Mas) dated to the eighteenth century and had been extended in the mid-nineteenth century and again in the mid-twentieth century. When we bought, the olive trees looked like overly healthy weeping willows, with the branches touching the ground. Similarly, the oleanders were so tall that they bent over the driveway creating a tunnel. It was magical, perfect for "hide and seek".

But, as anyone into gardening knows, pruning is the key to improving yield. So, on expert advice, we had seven years of excess growth removed. It was traumatic. They say that if an olive tree is properly pruned, a swallow can fly straight through it. In fact, we let them grow out a bit again, balancing aesthetics with productivity.

On the two hectares (roughly four acres), we had 256 olive trees, some several hundreds of years old, from which we produced oil. They were all Cailletier olives, rather small. We also had another 6 or 7 trees, including two Picholine, from which we brined the olives for eating.

Between 2008 and 2012, I participated in the harvests. We would "rake" the olives from the trees onto enormous nets spread out under the trees using handheld small rakes and a machine that looked like a rake with a long handle and vibrated to reach the higher branches. From the nets, we scooped up the olives and put them into plastic milk crates or cartons. Then, they are poured onto a screen over a blower that removes most of the leaves and twigs over the persons handling the cartons, with the olives landing back into another carton. Each carton held 10 kilos of olives.

The full crates were loaded into my Kangoo van, which could hold 15 crates if properly packed, and taken to the local mill 5 kilometers away—Le Moulin de la Brague. It would take 5 or 6 days with multiple trips on some days. Most years, we delivered between 2,500 and 3,500 kilos of olives (2-3 tons or more). I would do less and less of the work as the days went on, until all I could manage was driving the van and relying on two men at least 20 years older to unload at the Moulin, where they were poured through another stream of forced air.

The Moulin would press the olives daily on arrival. The oil from my olives was put into a 1000 liter container (one cubic meter) labeled "Beerbower." The oil rested for 2-3 months for the sediment to settle, then the amount I wanted was put into the bottles and containers I selected. We used 1/2, 1 and 5 liter containers, both glass and metal. We designed the label, produced in two sizes.

The rest of the oil would be purchased by the Moulin and sold under their label. In fact, I once saw it for sale in Gracious Hones on New York City's Upper Eastside.

My production ranged from 800 to 1400 liters, ignoring the year they flies ate the baby olives and the two years that late heavy rains knocked down the olives before the harvest. The December 2020 harvest was 3,127 kilograms of olives, which produced 410 kilograms or

447 liters of oil. The olive to oil yield was 13%. Pretty typical for our good years.

We normally harvested around December 1, when the olives are only partially ripe. The ripe ones are black, the less ripe are red/brown and the unripe are green. They made a very colorful mixture. Actually, beautiful in a basket. I aimed for a 25, 35, 40% mix, favoring green. That gives a slightly spicy, less buttery blend. Tastes apparently have been running to greener and greener oils.

By the way, for eating olives, you rinse them and pack them into a sealable container with a brine of half salt and half water. A very large amount of salt. Then, let it sit for at least 3 months. They keep forever. You will try eating an unbrined olive only once, no matter how ripe.

Notes on Labels

The designation "virgin" simply means oil from the first press of the olives. Virtually all oil for human consumption is "first press" or virgin. The statement "cold press" is meaningless. No one heats the press, and the pressing process inevitably generates heat. There is thought to be advantages to oil produced from just one variety of olive. Maybe some-one will market a blend of varieties, like with wine.

The quality issues with harvesting are the length of time the olives are left on the ground (only a couple of hours) and the delay in the pressing (preferably same day). Purists criticize the use of large machines that shake the whole tree, which are common with very large producers.

I do not know what it does to the olives, but I feel for the trees?

Amherst Changes

It has been some 56 years since I arrived at Amherst College as a freshman. Things have changed. As alumni, we mainly just watch. But, we cannot help but form judgments.

Of course, curricula change, and that is a matter above the pay grade of alumni. Same for faculty hiring and tenure decisions. But, there is more.

I

The decision to admit women was the first big change. I was initially ambivalent, for two reasons. First, we were hardly in the vanguard. If you do not lead change, it makes sense to stand back and evaluate, rather than just jump on the bandwagon. Second, I worried that the change could cost the College some of its specialness. In fact, the change was exceptionally well conceived and executed. The Trustees recognized that the preservation of the spirit of Amherst in a coed context would require a significant increase in enrollment, and they delivered what was needed.

II

The next change that drew my attention was the elimination of fraternities. I was skeptical for the same two reasons. This time, I think that the College threw out the baby with the bathwater. I understand, second hand, that the reckless and abusive behavior attributed to fraternities continues in their absence. But, the opportunities for the beneficial experiences offered by fraternities have not been replaced. The fraternities offered invaluable and unique exercises in group responsibility and of group decision-making and local politics. In some fraternities, there was significant diversity within the close association. These experiences are situations were not otherwise generally available. No substitutes were created. The College experience being offered was diminished as a result. I suspect that this mistake was the result of the polititization of the issue. The focus on the perceived evil blinded people to the good. Not uncommon. Indeed, arguably the prevailing method today.

III

In 2016, Amherst adopted a mascot. For many of us, Lord Jeff was thought to have been the College mascot; but, in 2016, we were told that it was only an unofficial mascot and that Lord Jeff was deemed unsuitable as a symbol of the College because of things he allegedly did in fighting Indians. It was somewhat curious. The names of buildings and streets were being changed around the country so as not to honor unacceptable historical figures; mascots for sports teams were being changed so as not to denigrate the groups named as mascots. But, Amherst changed its mascot so as not to honor him. Typically arrogant. Now, I do not care much about mascots, and the College did a nice job with the selection process for a new one.

I certainly do not miss the old College song, which was pretty stupid. But, I do think it a shame that the historic Lord Jeff Inn had to be renamed. I do not think we really needed a mascot. And, it is unfortunate that "The Warthogs" was already taken.

IV

More recently, Amherst and its President seem to have resisted the worst of the plague sweeping academia (I do not mean Covid), walking a fine line and preserving some dignity and, perhaps, integrity. However, I was extremely disappointed with the events concerning legacy admissions. I have no issue with the decision. Admission policies are the College's business, and they should be fluid and experimental, subject to continual adjustment.

I am stunned, however, by the decision to publicize the matter as a major policy change, as if it were a correction of some historic wrong. That implication is offensive, hurtful and false. The disclosure was relatively neutral, but the nature of the following publicity was readily predictable in today's climate. One cannot help but think that there was an intentional effort to pander to certain current popular sentiments and score cheap "Brownie points" at the expense of a large group of alumni.

Legacy admissions were good for Amherst and its students. It added balance to the student body and increased the sense of tradition. My class was certainly better and stronger because of the presence of the so-called legacies. They were certainly not all wealthy or privileged. They played a part in the enrichment of the lives of they families and communities.

But, the most distressing thing is that the College has limited its future options and flexibility. A self-inflicted injury, and for what?

The Trustees and the President have a duty to take the longer view. To rise above the current passions and fashions. To stand up for the good and lasting.

So,

we watch and contemplate;

perhaps,

we revisit our estate plans.

To Reproduce or Not?

I have been thinking about the valid reasons one would want to have children. Of course, my comments about things applicable primarily to mothers are admittedly just speculation.

First, there is something meaningful about participating in fundamental human experiences. Child bearing is probably just behind being born and dying. I think one would be just curious about it, and about what it means. Of course, this consideration is largely for women. (I think that men can have an emotional and psychological interest in reproducing. Certainly, most of us have a biological impulse to procreate.)

It is also a life affirming act, although certainly not the only one.

For both parents, there is the experience of unconditional love, giving and receiving. And, the overwhelming sense of dependency and protectiveness: The unquestioning readiness to give your own life to save your child. I gather one can find these feelings with other than a biological offspring, but I did not. They are worthy experiences.

Then, there is the related experience of commitment.

"After his birth, ...[I]nstantly it became clear that the life of the child has infinite dignity. Of course it is worth the grief, even if the candle is only lit for such a short time. Once a kid is born you've been seized by a commitment, the strength of which you couldn't even have imagined beforehand. It brings you to the doorstep of disciplined service."

David Brooks, The Second Mountain. p.58.

Of course, there is also the opportunity to fashion one's own family and holiday traditions. To recreate one's childhood the way it should have been. This does not require biological offspring, but it does require children. One can join someone else's family for a particular holiday on a regular basis, but that would be difficult for all holidays.

Parenting is a profound learning experience, and a humbling, confusing one. Again, it need not be the parenting of one's biological offspring.

And, there is the prospect of grandchildren, which is a special and rewarding experience, but there is a long wait.

What else?

Children provide someone to whom you can leave possessions of special significance. Of course, they may not want them.

Similarly risky reasons to have children are (i) to have someone to take care of you as you age or (ii) to discover what your genes transmit. Both have potential for serious disappointment.

POLITICS

A "Political" Viewpoint?

"[T]he essence of politics:
the ability to reflect consciously
on different directions one's society could take,
and to make explicit arguments why
it should take one path rather than another."

David Graeber
The Dawn of Everything:
A New History of Humanity
(2022) p. 86

As I have been doing more solitary observing and thinking, I am realizing the extent to which certain beliefs (which some would call prejudices) influence my reactions. So, I have tried to sort out and organize these beliefs. I believe that the following propositions are true:

I.

All people act in pursuit of their own self-interest, as they perceive it.

Most people are inherently lazy; they will take the path of least resistance. Their default position is idleness.

Yet, many people are capable of great ingenuity, commitment and hard work if there are rewards available for successful endeavors, whether such rewards are wealth or fame or power.

As a result, the structure of incentives people face—the rewards and punishments, the opportunities and obstacles—is an important determinant of people's behavior.

However, people vary greatly in aptitude, drive, abilities and effectiveness as a result of genetic inheritance and upbringing. There are only relatively few at the top performance level found in almost every type of endeavor.

II.

Human happiness and well-being benefit from traditions (even dumb ones): a sense of a history and of continuity, as well as a sense of community, of belonging and of being part of something bigger than one's self. These are the things that give direction to life and provide the constraints and boundaries that inevitably shape one's life, whether one goes with the flow or strives to burst the banks.

"The customs of the institution structure the soul,
making it easier to be good. They guide behavior gently
along certain time-tested lines. By practicing the customs
of an institution, we are not alone; we are admitted into a
community that transcends time."

David Brooks, *The Road to Character* (2015), p.116.

"People who look backward to see the heroism and the struggle
that came before see themselves as debtors who owe something,
who have some obligation to pay it forward."
David Brooks, *The Second Mountain* (2019) p.283.

Work is good for a person. It reduces idle time, and its temptations, and provides a sense of independence and identity.

Charitable acts are beneficial to the doer. The acts themselves foster empathy and help create the sense of belonging. Of course, they also enhance the community.

> "[L]ife is defined by commitments and obligations.
> The life well lived is a journey from open options
> to sweet compulsions."
> Brooks, *The Second Mountain*, p.56.

III.

Bureaucracies are like people—their top priority is self-preservation and they tend to get fatter over time.

In most organizations, some 20% of the people do 80% of the work. Less than 10% of the people generate most of the value.

The world is exceedingly complex. Most plans will go wrong. Intended consequences will often not be realized; unexpected consequences will almost always intrude and will often overwhelm the best laid plans. The broader the scope, the greater the change and/or the longer the time horizon of the plan, the greater the likely error.

Decentralized decision-making minimizes the impact of errors and bad judgment, while allowing successes to be copied and, thereby, to multiply. It brings decisions closer to the matters at issue. Decentralization also allows diversity, promotes innovation and experimentation and encourages the taking of responsibility.

Effective exercise of responsibility requires personal accountability. If a position has room (or a need) for excellence or improvement and is one in which mediocrity is not sufficient, then there need to be personal rewards and consequences, incentives and discipline, selection and selectivity in order to realize the potential that is there.

The biggest disadvantages of bureaucracies, of unions and of the civil service are that they all diminish accountability, protect incompetence and stifle initiative. Such organizations are adequate only for positions as to which people are fungible, where the job requirements and opportunities are within the reach of almost everyone, among whom some will struggle, some will be comfortable and some will lean back and contentedly vegetate.

The possession of power over people or things or events is both addictive and corrupting.

Government seems to invite corruption. It comes with the power to grant benefits, which power corrupts.

Government largesse, conversely, seems always to be accompanied by fraud. Temptations are just too great, probably because stealing from bureaucrats with no personal accountability is so easy, possibly because there seem to be no real victims.

(Look at Social Security fraud, whether stealing one's neighbor's benefit checks or collecting checks for your deceased relatives. Or, Medicare fraud by doctors and other health care providers. The pandemic relief programs have been fraught with fraudulent claims for unemployment benefits, PPP loans, and small business relief, as even acknowledged now by the *Washington Post* and the President.)

"The IG [Inspector General] ... "found more than 70,000 suspicious loans, totaling $4.6 billion. The report calls the level of fraud 'unprecedented'... .' ...The IG has also flagged about $80 billion in suspicious transactions via another SBA pandemic program, Economic Injury Disaster Loans. The fraud in Covid unemployment benefits was possibly worse... . The Labor Department's IG has estimated that 'at least $163 billion in pandemic UI benefits could have been paid improperly, with a significant portion attributable to fraud.'"

The Editorial Board,
"Covid Fraudsters Are Still At Large,"
WSJ.com, June 7, 2022

"Many who participated in what prosecutors are calling the largest fraud in U.S. history — the theft of hundreds of billions of dollars in taxpayer money intended to help those harmed by the coronavirus pandemic — couldn't resist purchasing luxury automobiles. Also mansions, private jet flights and swanky vacations. ...[W]hat experts say is the theft of as much as $80 billion ... of the $800 billion handed out in a Covid relief plan known as the Paycheck Protection Program, or PPP. That's on top of the $90 billion to $400 billion believed to have been stolen from the $900 billion Covid unemployment relief program — at least half taken by international fraudsters... . And another $80 billion potentially pilfered from a separate Covid disaster relief program."

Ken Dilanian and Laura Strickler,
"'Biggest fraud in a generation':
The looting of the Covid relief plan known as PPP"
NBC News, March 28, 2022

One should be scared of majority rule, if not buffeted and moderated by lobbyists, influential people and groups with agendas and an independent media.

"The democratic political sphere can turn into one in which the logic is not cooperation and growth but rather confiscation and re-distribution—with 'deserving' and 'undeserving' standing in, respectively, for the friends and enemies of the powerful."

J. Bradford DeLong, *Slouching Towards Utopia:*
An Economic History of the Twentieth Century (2022), p.93

But, one should be even more frightened of government by experts and unaccountable bureaucrats or by an unfettered President.

SO ...

These beliefs color my opinions on most matters, in combination with a strong commitment to tolerance and individual liberty. And, I can see how these propositions provide a basis for a conservative polit-ical view. Presumably, this view is a result of upbringing and, perhaps, genetics.

"Some people seem **to have been born into this world with a sense of indebtedness for the blessing of being alive.** They are aware of the transmission of generations, what has been left to them by those who came before, their indebtedness to their ancestors, **their obligations to a set of moral responsibilities that stretch across time.**"

Brooks, *The Road to Character*, p.126 (emphasis added)

Un-Equal-Ity

"Unequal" is the norm in our world. We find "not equal" things every where—not equal in size, in ability, in attractiveness, in resources, in living and in dying. As they say, it is only in death that we are all equal.

Yet, we find ourselves surrounded by protests about "inequality," identifying it as a matter of significant societal concern. "Inequality" suggests unfairness or impropriety. The same seems not so for "unequal". Curious, since they are simply a noun and an adjective for the same concept. The spelling difference appears because the prefix "un" comes from old English, while the noun comes from the French (which came from the Latin). There are similar examples, like unable and inability or ungrateful and ingratitude. Even in those examples, the adjective seems only to state a plain fact, while the noun invokes the image of a state of affairs, with some overtones of moral judgment (or is it just me).

So, I will use the word unequality for this discussion. The meaning is the same (and, I am assured by *Merriam-Webster*, it is proper English), but I do so in the hope of making the discussion somewhat more neutral.

[For convenience, I quote myself below, rather than rewrite the points.]

Unequal Wealth (and Income)

As I previously wrote: "[t]he branch of human 'knowledge' known as economics has ancient roots, reflecting man's long-standing interest in trade and money (media of exchange). But, then, we see in the eighteenth century a new focus on two rather distinct questions: Why are certain nations richer than others, even when one controls for natural resources? Why are diamonds—intrinsically useless—worth more than water—an essential of life?" *Important Things We Don't Know About Nearly Everything* (2022), p.122.

These were new questions at the time, arising from rather recent events in human history.

> "**Most people of a few centuries ago led lives comparable to those of their remote ancestors**—and most other individuals around the globe—millennia ago, ...[For] the entirety of human history up until the recent dramatic leap forward [,] **the fruits of technological advancements were channelled primarily towards larger and denser populations** and had only a glacial impact on their long-term prosperity."

Oded Galor,
The Journey of Humanity: The Origins of Wealth and Inequality
(2022), pp.3-4 (emphasis added).

Then came the Age of Industrialization. As I have previously written: "some striking insights were achieved into causes of increased productivity and growth. Adam Smith [in his *Wealth of Nations* (1776)] identified the importance of the division of labor and specialization, attributing much of the progress and promise of industrialized economies to the **benefits that were derived from the increasing division of labor that greater scale and free trade would enable.** The benefits of the specialization ... include improved skill at the task at hand resulting from repetition, improved techniques that may be discovered as a result of the greater experience gained..., new technology made feasible as a result of the increases scale of the process at issue, reduced time and resources spent in frequently changing tasks, efficiencies in training for specialized jobs and, even, the opportunities to capture differences in relative differential abilities in performing particular tasks through trade; although, the full theory of 'comparative advantage' awaited David Ricardo, 50 years later." *Important Things*, pp.122-3 (emphasis added).

Following the Industrial Revolution of the nineteenth century, economic progress exploded. As J. Bradford DeLong writes:

"[T]he watershed-crossing events of around 1870—**the triple emergence of globalization, the industrial research lab, and the modern corporation** ushered in changes that began **to pull the world out of the dire poverty that had been humanity's lot for the previous ten thousand years,** since the discovery of agriculture. ...Today, the luckier economies of the world have achieved levels of per capita prosperity at least twenty times those of 1870, and at least twenty-five times those of 1770... ."

Slouching Towards Utopia:
An Economic History of the Twentieth Century
(2022), pp.1, 11 (emphasis added).

And, the wealth accumulation among nations was very unequal and has continued so. For example, today, with about 5% of the world's population, the United States holds some 30% of the world's wealth. (In the United States today, the top 1% of households hold about 30% of the wealth.)

In his recent book, Oded Galor has summarized what he found in his research as the causes of the differences in wealth and economic growth among nations. There are many. Several clearly apply to countries—

geography (absence of tse-tse flies and malaria carrying mosquitoes, fertile soil, East/West orientation, suitable climate, abundant and diverse local plant life, access to navigable waters), political structure (decentralized, public participation), legal structure (stable and robust property rights, enforceability of contracts, relative security for people and property). But, several others describe characteristics of societies and people —future-oriented, competitive, risk tolerant, committed to investment in human capital (care of children, good nutrition, education, training), trusting of others (promoting trade and the exchange of knowledge), relative gender equality (women in the workforce), genetic and cultural diversity (conducive to the generation of new ideas).

(We might find here some insight into why certain communities, like certain nations, are notably less prosperous than others. In his lists, for example, it is pretty easy to spot things not generally found in isolated urban ghetto communities.)

In contrast, Thomas Piketty endorses:

> "Ken Pomeranz's study, published in 2000, on the 'great divergence' between Europe and China in the eighteenth and nineteenth centuries, [that] ... the development of Western industrial capitalism is closely linked to systems of **the international division of labor, the frenetic exploitation of natural resources, and the European powers' military and colonial domination over the rest of the planet.**"

> Thomas Piketty, *A Brief History of Equality*
> (2022), p.3 (emphasis added).*

This theory addresses part of the rise of the Western colonial powers, like Britain, France and Spain, but not the more general phenomenon of economic growth that proceeded and followed that rise and occurred elsewhere. Indeed, DeLong explains that even during the nineteenth century, "[p]opulation growth ate the benefits of invention and innovation in technology and organization, leaving only the exploitative upper class noticeably better off." *Slouching Towards Utopia*, p.30. Yet,

> "[a]fter 1870, sending a family member across the ocean to work became a possibility open to all save the very poorest of European households. And humans responded by the millions. ...[M]igration did not raise wages much in the ... economies of China and India. Both had such substantial populations that emigration was a drop in the bucket. **Through misfortune and bad government, India and China had failed to escape the shackles of the Malthusian Devil** [population growth consuming increases in productivity]."

> *Id.*, pp.40, 44.**

Adam Smith's answer to the second question (supply and demand) led to the development of Neo-classical economic theory purporting to explain how markets work. Consistent with that theory, was what happened next. "The growth of trade meant that the logic of comparative advantage could be deployed to its limit. ...And so the surge in real wages was worldwide, not confined to where industrial technologies were then being deployed. This was the consequence of finance and trade following labor." DeLong, *Slouching Towards Utopia*,, pp.49, 50. "The market economy enables the astonishing coordination and cooperation of by now nearly eight billion humans in a highly productive division of labor." *Id.*, p.13. Moreover, "[t]he unique American advantage was greatly reinforced by the fact that in the United States, the period of explosive prosperity set in motion around 1870 ... lasted without interruption longer than elsewhere in the world. China collapsed into revolution in 1911. Europe descended into the hell of World War I in 1914." *Id.*, pp.78-9.

Now, 250 years later, attention has focused on the differences in the wealth of individuals, a subject on which Neo-classical economics had indirectly offered an explanation not now considered acceptable.

See, Joseph E. Stiglitz, *The Price of Inequality: How Today's Divided Society Endangers Our Future* (2013), p.30 ("The theory that came to dominate, beginning in the second half of the nineteenth century—and still does—was called 'marginal productivity theory'; those with higher productivities earned higher incomes that reflected their greater contribution to society"). The Noble Prize winning economist argues that:

> "**Technology and scarcity, working through the ordinary laws of supply and demand, play a role in shaping today's inequality,** but something else is at work, and **that something else is government.** Inequality is the result of political forces as much as of economic ones. ...[A]nother way to get rich. You can simply **arrange for the government to hand you cash.** ...A little-noticed change in legislation ... can reap billions of dollars. ...[A]lmost every law has distributive consequences, with some groups benefiting, typically at the expense of others."

Id., pp.30, 48, 58 (emphasis added).

With his conclusion applied to today. I whole heartedly agree. The difference is that Stiglitz views it as a compelling reason for more government, while I view it as a compelling reason for less.

Stiglitz goes on:

> "[W]e have a political system that gives inordinate power to those at the top, and they have used that power not only to limit the extent of redistribution but also to shape the rules of the game in their favor, and to **extract from the public what can only be called large 'gifts.'** Economists ... call them **rent seeking ,getting income not as a reward to creating wealth but by grabbing a larger share of the wealth** that would otherwise have been produced without their effort."

Id., pp.31 (emphasis added).

He concludes "..Those at the top have learned how to suck out money from the rest in ways that the rest are hardly aware of—that is their true innovation." *Id.*, p.32.

"[T]heir true innovation"?

Really?

Ignoring the hyperbole, I agree that much of the wealth in this country is attributable to "economic rents", but I think Stiglitz unfairly characterizes and stigmatizes that phenomenon. Economic rent arises from scarcity. When there are few of something that many people (or a few wealthy people) want, the price will be bid up until it is determined who wins the prize. The cost of production (whether average or marginal cost) of the desired product is irrelevant, because the supply of the product cannot be increased, at least in the short run (if can be increased in the long run, we may have "quasi rent" in the short run). Such rent plays an indispensable role in the allocation of scarce resources.

Stiglitz is misleading in his repeated assertion that the receipt of rent takes money away from others. It does so only in the sense that the persons paying the rents might have spent that money on something else if they had not paid the rent.

Take some examples. A football player may have little value to society, but differential pay is a way to allocate the players among teams and will reflect the players' relative values to the owners. The result is stupendous income for some, in the form of "rent". The same market mechanism works for CEOs, babysitters, caregivers and skilled tradesmen. Celebrities receive rent for their performances. Many, many others would eagerly take their roles for far less (even for no pay), but the producer chooses to pay millions for the star.

Economists call that rent, but that does not mean the star does not deserve it or that the star has taken (or to use Stiglitz' preferred verbs in this context, "grabbed" or "sucked out") money from your pocket or mine. We pay willingly. (Some pay eagerly.)

CONSEQUENCES OF UNEQUALITY

What are the consequences today of past disparities in the distribution of wealth among nations but, more importantly, among individuals within nations? Significant concentrations of wealth have given us art, music and grand architecture: cathedrals, castles, palaces and stately homes and gardens. Some monumental architecture was the result of collaborative community effort, but much of our rich cultural heritage is a result of the ambitions, egotism and patronage of the very wealthy. Of course, another consequence is some part of the unequality of wealth that exists today (but, probably only a modest part, as I discuss in the essay on mobility).

So, what are the consequences today of today's wealth unequality? For one thing, the world is more diverse, colorful and interesting because of unequality. Although I will never own one, I am glad that exotic cars exit. The same for luxury yachts, private planes, haut couture, handmade watches and fine jewelry. I am glad that skilled artisans still exist. And, even fashion designers. Not to forget expensive wines and glamorous hotels and palatial houses.

In addition, and very importantly, the possibility of wealth unequality provides the incentives for saving and investment, as well as for entrepreneurship and innovation. Another consequence is huge amounts of private philanthropy: creative, experimental and idiosyncratic. Such private undertakings have a far different impact than government programs. Admittedly, there is also obscene waste and tasteless excess. But, that still seems better than bland, stifling uniformity to me.

What about unequality of income? The possibility of such unequality creates incentives for innovation, hard work and risk taking. Income unequality also rewards skill and ability, as well as blind luck. And, as noted above, unequality of income through economic rent is a means of allocating unique or scarce resources. In addition, such unequality spurs capital formation ,since the higher income recipients save much more of their income than the lower income recipients do.

There is a close relationship between unequality of wealth and unequality of income, obviously. The consequences of both are similar. One consequence I have not mentioned is influence, of all kinds. But, we may be especially concerned about political. The remedy for that problem are rules concerning campaign finance and diligence to prevent corruption.

In a 2012 speech cited by Stigliz, then Chairman of the Council of Ecnomic Advisers Alan Krueger identified "potential [adverse] consequences of rising inequality for the economy":

1. "...as inequality rises, the prospects for intergenerational mobility fall [an alleged phenomenon that he dubs "The Great Gatsby Curve"].
2. ...rising inequaity and slow income growth encourag[e] many families to borrow beyond their means to try to maintain their consumption.
3. .. [rising inequality and slow income growth] reduc[e] aggregate consumption....if another $1.1 trillion had been earned by the bottom 99% instead of the top 1%, annual consumption would be about $440 billion higher.
4. ...in a society where income inequality is greater, political decisions are likely to result in policies that lead to less growth.

5.   ...wage discrepancies can be bad for employee morale and productivity. ... a more fair distribution of wages ... would raise morale and productivity."

"The Rise and Consequences of Inequality in the United States," *Council of Economic Advisers*, January 12, 2012.

Well, pretty thin stuff. The evidence for the first assertion is based on relative, not absolute, mobility and does not establish the direction of any causation anyway. Not much to say about the second, except there is no proof that it is true. In any event, it is a poor reason to promote equality. The third consequence is more likely a benefit of unequality, not a harm, if one favors growth. The fourth contradicts the third and is unsupported. The fifth is simply not relevant to the issue here concerning the gap between the top and the bottom.

Of course, one may recognize the desirability (and inevitability) of unequality, but still ask how much is enough or can there be too much. Unfortunately, there is no answer to either question, and the evidence from historical and international comparisons is only suggestive, at best.

UNEQUALITY IN THE UNITED STATES

So, let's look at some of the facts about unequality in the U.S.

Although, it is hard to find a good measure, it is generally agreed that unequality in the United States dramatically decreased from 1928 through 1945, then leveled off until the late 1970s. Some 50 years. The next 15 years saw some upward movement; then, it appears to have increased sporadically again after 1986.*** In 2010, by one measure, the United States was less unequal than France, Germany and Italy and similar to Sweden, Poland, Spain, Japan and the United Kingdom in income before taxes and government transfers. When taxes and transfers are taken into account, it becomes more unequal. Alan B. Krueger, "The Rise and Consequences of Inequality in the United States," Council of Economic Advisers, January 12, 2012, Fig.11.

However, there are disagreements about which "transfers" to include.

'In 2017, federal, state and local governments redistributed $2.8 trillion, or 22% of the nation's earned household income. **More than two-thirds of those transfer payments went to households in the bottom two income quintiles. Remarkably the Census Bureau chooses to count only $900 billion of that $2.8 trillion as income for the recipients.** Excluded from **the measurement of household income is some $1.9 trillion of government transfers.** These include the earned-income tax credit, whose beneficiaries get a check from the Treasury; food stamps, which let beneficiaries buy food with government issued debit cards; and numerous other programs... .'

Phil Gramm and John Early,
"Incredible Shrinking Income Inequality"
WSJ.com, March 23, 2021 (emphasis added).

When corrected to reflect total government benefits, the measurement shows a continuing decline in unequality after 1986. *Id.* Moreover,

"[I]n the bottom quintile, there are on average only 1.92 people living in a household. The second and middle quintiles have 2.41 and 2.62 people respectively. After adjusting income for the number of people living in the household, ...[t]he blockbuster finding is that **on a per capita basis the average bottom quintile household received 14% more income than the average second-quintile household and 3.3% more than the average middle-income household.**"

Phil Gramm and John Early,
"Income Equality, Not Inequality, Is the Problem"
WSJ.com, August 29, 2022 (emphasis added).

There is a lot of talk about the top 1%, some about the top 0.1%, but the real action is with the top 0.01%—a mere 16,000 households. That is where the enormous increases are occurring and is the principal source of the growing unequality. Most other measures of unequality are actually rather misleading, because of the impact of this tiny group. Much of the wealth of this group is attributable to the rapid appreciation of equities and other assets in general, but a lot of it reflects the staggering successes of businesses that members started or supported with an investment early.

And, most of that wealth consists of unrecognized gains, so it would not yet have been considered income. (There are some pretty significant disconnects between wealth and income.) This wealth is also rather transitory, in reality. The market value may drop. If the stock is sold, income taxes will be paid; if (when) the holder dies, either the stock will go to charity or some 40% will go to the government in estate taxes.

For perspective, about half of U.S. households have negative or nominal net worths (less than $10,000, excluding home ownership), the top 1% have net worths in excess of $11 million, the top 0.1% have net worths over $40 million and the top 0.01%, from over $100 million to $260 billion. The top 0.01% hold roughly half the wealth of the top 0.1%, which in turn hold roughly half of the wealth of the top 1.0% (the top 10 % actually hold about 40% of the total wealth of all households).

As for income, households in the top 1% have incomes in excess of $500,000, while the top 0.1% have incomes in excess of $3 million and the top 0.01% have incomes ranging from $8 million well into the hundreds of millions. This top income category generally includes a number of professional athletes, a lot of entertainers and CEOs, some lawyers, a bunch of investment bankers and fund managers and a couple of lottery winners. Many of these will be in the top net worth category as well, but not all. There is much greater disparity in net worth than in income.

Now, all of these numbers are estimates, but they indicate the nature and magnitude of the relationships. So, what does this all mean?

SOME HYPOTHETICALS

Consider:

The average U.S. household income is now about $98,000 a year. The median (the midpoint) is about $68,000 a year. If one imagines that half the income of the top 10% were received instead by the bottom 10%, both the average and the median would stay the same.

If one imagines that income were allocated equally, the average would still not change, but the median would equal the average, since that would be the income of every household. In addition, if the income of the top 10% were simply cut in half, then average income would go down about 10%, the median income would stay the same. In comparison, if the income of the bottom 20% were to double, then average income would go up, median income would still be unchanged. In these examples, of course, unequality would be reduced.

If all of the wealth of the top 1% were distributed equally among the 99%, everyone would get a one time payment of about $14,000. Would that permanently change their world?

Finally, suppose the net worth of all households were equalized and income of all households were to be made the same for three years, but all of our institutions were to remain the same, what would happen after the three years? I suggest that unequality would start to increase and would do so rapidly and exponentially. Moreover, I suspect that before long, many, maybe most, households would again be in the same quintile they were in just before this experiment began, both by income and by net worth. Indeed, even Thomas Piketty seems to agree that redistribution will not accomplish much. *See A Brief History of Equality*, p.164.**

If our institutions were changed to prevent this result, I think that total national income would fall dramatically, bringing down both the averages and the medians.

Yet, Stiglitz says:

"[T]hose at the top are **grabbing** an increasing fraction of the nation's income—so much of a larger share that what's left over for the rest is diminished.... There's been **redistribution away from the bottom and middle,** and almost all of what's been redistributed has gone to the very top, the top 1 percent. This is **a direct corollary** of the fact that incomes at the bottom and in the middle have been falling, while those at the very top have been rising."

Id., pp.25, 298 (emphasis added).

Apparently taking a cue from Paul Krugman (who became a leading *New York Times* columnist through arrogant sarcasm, exaggeration and the hurling of insults), Stiglitz abandons any pretense of objectivity in his choice of words to express this conclusion. But, he also abandons logic. The fact that the wealth or income of the top 1% goes up at the same time that the wealth or income of the bottom 20% goes down simply does not mean that money was taken by one group from the other or even moved from one to the other. It is not a corollary.

For example, your raise is likely not the cause of or even related to the decline in my income (I retired). Suppose the stock market soars, as it has during the last five years. People who own stock become wealthier. People who do not own stock become relatively less wealthy, but their actual wealth does not go down. Nothing was "grabbed" from them. Now, suppose that government blunders result in rapid inflation, as has happened in the last year. The bottom half's real income goes down, not because the income of the top 1% has gone up. The wealth of the debtors goes up, that of the savers goes down. Over the first six months of 2022, stock prices fell, decreasing the wealth at the top. Are the poor better off?

Another example. Suppose that housing prices go up, with the prices for luxury properties rising much faster than prices for the average homes, as has happened over the last three years. All homeowners are wealthier. The family that can now sell their mansion for $11 million, having bought it for $5 million five years ago, is certainly now wealthier, but not at the expense of the owners of average homes (unless you believe that there is a fixed amount of money that will spent on housing, which was "sucked up" by the sellers of mansions).

Well?

CONCLUSIONS

It seems to me that all of this suggests rather strongly that much of today's political rhetoric is seriously misdirected. The matter for concern and for action is not the 1% or the more important top 0.01%; it is the behavior of the bottom 50%. Why do they not save, why do they not invest? Increases in income will not change the picture materially without changes in spending habits. People need to work "on the books" so they accrue Social Security benefits. They need to contribute to retirement plans. They need to use credit cards carefully. And, they need to believe in a future.

Curiously, during the pandemic, savings by the bottom half went up. Why? For many, the relief payments and loan suspensions were a complete windfall. The money may have been saved because of fear and uncertainty, because of lock downs and because future payments were an unknown. It appears that spending is now increasing in 2022 and savings are decreasing. An increase in income will make little lasting difference absent a corresponding increase in net worth. An increase in net worth will make little difference if it is transitory, that is, if it is just spent.

I do not mean to suggest that emergency relief is not helpful or not necessary. It is both. But, it should be deemed to be temporary and transitional, even if the transition may take a long time. Financial aid programs should either be explicitly of limited term or contain a plan for a transition to its termination for each included individual or family.

There are government actions that could promote the changes that would help make a difference and reduce inequality. For example, instead of the current Earned Income Credit, we could pay $5 per hour for all hours worked that are reflected in a W-2 to each person with an income below $40,000 a year. We could match contributions made to a traditional IRA, taxable only upon withdrawal. We could offer subsidies for the teaching of "home economics" and financial management. There are many possibilities for programs that encourage constructive behavior and that do not reward those who do not try.

So, it seems that unequality is pervasive and inevitable. It is also beneficial, providing much of the "spice" in life. This is especially true for unequality in wealth. Thus, we should not obsess about the top 16,000 households making up the top .01% (or even the top 1%). We should not focus on the actions of the tail but on the health of the dog. Public policy should strive to create the opportunities for everyone to achieve healthy, constructive lives. And, of course, everyone should pay their taxes and abide by the law.

But, for context, remember:

"[A]t least since the end of the eighteenth century there has been a historical movement toward equality. The world of the early 2020s, no matter how unjust it may seem, is more egalitarian than that of 1950 or that of 1900, which were themselves in many respects more egalitarian than those of 1850 or 1780."

Piketty, *A Brief History of Equality*, pp. 1-2.

---

* Thomas Piketty insists that the significant global trend toward wealth equality from 1915 to 1980 was due to the emergence of the welfare state and progressive taxation ("progressive taxation, as it functioned in the course of the twentieth century, enabled us not only to more fairly distribute taxes on wealth and income but also to impose narrow limits on inequalities before taxes"). *A Brief History of Equality*, p.157. Yet, he describes the tremendous amounts of private wealth that were lost as a result of WW I, the Great Depression, the collapse of the colonial empires, WW II and the cancelation of massive public debt in Western Europe. In the U.S., the welfare state improved the standard of living of the recipients, but did little for their wealth or their futures; progressive taxation reduced the after-tax incomes of some of the top 10%, but it also caused alterations in how people were compensated or received earnings and resulted in the diversion of resources to tax avoidance, reducing reported taxable income among the well off. (By the way, I am in favor of progressive taxation. I previously set out my proposal for tax reform in the United States. It would result in a much more progressive structure with a broader base.)

** DeLong describes his conclusions about the impact on wages of the migration of some 1 out of every 7 people in the world following 1870. The immigrants generally found the higher wages for which they had immigrated; the laborers staying behind saw their real wages rise as the local labor supply shrank, except in China and India; in the Northern, industrialized countries, wages in general went up, despite the increase in the supply of labor; but, in the Southern, agricultural countries where most of the Chinese and Indian immigrants went, the wages were suppressed by the influx of workers willing to work for very little. Overall, the dramatic increase in the mobility of goods and of resources, including labor, enabled by the plummeting costs of transportation, pursuant to the law of comparative advantage, delivered large improvements in the living standards of the working classes across the world.

Id., pp.44-50.

*** "Redistribution of property alone does not suffice to transcend capitalism [,]... simply to replace large property owners with small and middle-sized property owners who are just as greedy and careless of the social and environmental consequences of their actions... ." So, he advocates for much more dramatic changes in the existing economic/political systems. He rejects authoritarian alternatives (like Stalinism and contemporary China), favoring "a new form of democratic socialism: self-managing, decentralized, and based on the continual circulation of power and property [by which he means regularly imposed redistributions of wealth]." *Id.*, pp.166-167. Yet, he acknowledges that: "[t[he internal organization of these quasi-state, hypercentralized authorities is not at all clear, ... how they might function in a truly democratic and emancipatory way. It would be premature, to say the least, to assume ... that any **risk of bureaucratic and authoritarian excess** can be ruled out."

Id., p.169 (emphasis added).

"The Beloved Community"

Because it was discussed in a series at my church, The Old Presbyterian Meeting House, I read *A More Perfect Union: A New Vision for Building the Beloved Community* (2022) by Adam Russell Taylor. I write about it here, because it is in front of me and is the most expensive Kindle book I ever bought.

Taylor begins by noting the importance of "framing", how the way a question or issue is presented or framed can affect how it is answered or perceived. Then, he goes on to frame his discussion quite aggressively to create his narrative.

His thesis is that "America can never fully thrive as an idea or a shared political, social, and economic project without us choosing to become one people." He says, "The pressing question is this: Is America truly a people in addition to being a nation? Or do our ethnic and racial identities and divisions make it impossible to identify as a common people with shared values, aspirations, and experiences?" One people? That sounds good, but what does it mean in practice?

I have expressed my assessment of "systematic racism" elsewhere. Taylor did not alter my view.

Yet...

There are some specific points I feel are worth addressing.

1. Taylor cites approvingly the argument from Ibram X. Kendi's book How to Be an Antiracist that the opposite of racist is not non-racist but anti-racist. "What's the difference?" Kendi asks.

"One endorses either the idea of a racial hierarchy as a racist, or racial equality as an antiracist. One either believes problems are rooted in groups of people, as a racist, or locates the roots of problems in power and policies, as an antiracist. One either allows racial inequities to persevere, as a racist, or confronts racial inequities, as an antiracist."

Thus, it is not sufficient not to discriminate and not to feel prejudice; not to be racist requires that one be opposed to and seek to eliminate racism. Activism is required. We must not just be good, but must make others good too. That seems like a prescription for meddling and for coercion: we should all be part of a kind "Neighborhood Watch" to keep an eye on each other. That is not a very Christian idea.

2. Then, Taylor goes on to explain, "one of the most challenging aspects of building the Beloved Community is repenting and making amends for the deep wounds. ...This necessarily includes intentional amends through some form of reparations for the legacy of slavery." (Emphasis added.) Reparations? Certainly, the victims who were enslaved deserved some compensation, but it is too late for that. Would reparations or amends today be made as penance or recompense?

Taylor notes:

"The case for reparations is often tied to all the ways in which 246 years of legal slavery served as the backbone in building America's wealth, well as to the specific promise made by General William T.

Sherman at the end of the Civil War to grant "forty acres and a mule" to every surviving family of slavery, a promissory note that was quickly reversed by President Andrew Johnson after the assassination of President Lincoln."

But,

- The first reason might have been persuasive in 1850, when the factual assertion would have been accurate, but that wealth was destroyed in the Civil War. Slavery was not the source of the wealth of the United States in 1920 or in 2022. There may be some property that was taken from or is attributable to slaves, but that is very case specific.
- The alleged "promissory note" never existed. Such a long-term commitment could not have been validly created by General Sherman as a war time executive order, only by an act of Congress. The "40 acres and a mule" was proposed as a means of assisting the former slaves to become self sufficient and independent. It is a tragedy that it did not happen. We would likely have had a stronger country if it had. (The equivalent today would be education.)
- As a matter of compensation, it could never be enough to eliminate the resentment or quell demands for more.
- If the goal is restitution (to put the descendants of slaves in the position that they would have been in but for slavery), few of them would agree to be so treated today. They would be living in Africa or the Caribbean with average incomes of about 10% of what they earn here or receive in government benefits. Indeed, there are billions of people in the world world who eagerly change places with them and millions who would risk their lives to do so.
- Penance? Was not the Civil War penance on an unprecedented scale?

The Christian thing would be to forgive, especially the "sins of the fathers".

3. Taylor invokes the early Church, presumably as an example to follow: "In scripture there are countless glimpses into God's preferred future. In Acts 2 and 4, the Apostle Paul paints a picture of the Beloved Community in the early church, where resources are shared, everyone is cared for, and multiethnic, multilingual, and multinational community takes shape." However, the earliest Christians believed that the world was about to end, that Judgment Day was at hand. People behave differently when they think they are about to die. Watch the movie On the Beach (preferably the 1960 version in black and white). Of course, the Church struggled when confronted with the lack of the imminent end.

4. Taylor discusses the founding myths of America and how to change them. Citing Richard T. Hughes, Taylor asserts:

"Hughes identifies five myths that emerged in specific periods of American history; to varying degrees, each flourishes today, often in combination with others. While most of these myths hold a kernel of truth and offer the potential for good, in the absolutizing and distorting of them, Americans have often undermined the potential virtues that otherwise stood at their respective cores."

These myths are:

- "The Myth of a Chosen Nation—the notion that God Almighty chose the United States for a special mission in the world.
- The Myth of Nature's Nation—the conviction that American ideals and institutions are rooted in the natural order, that is, in God's own intentions first revealed at the dawn of civilization.

- The Myth of the Millennial Nation—the notion that the United States, building on that natural order, will usher in a final golden age for all humankind.
- The Myth of a Christian Nation—the claim that America is a Christian nation, consistently guided by Christian values.
- The Myth of the Innocent Nation—the conviction that, while other nations may have blood on their hands, the nobility of the American cause always redeems the nation and renders it innocent."

The difficulties here are that while each of these myths appeared with some force in the course of our history (from the first Puritans in the 17th century to Woodrow Wilson in 1917), none has much of any traction today. They are a part of our history, a part of which we should be aware. But, ask people today is America the nation "that God Almighty chose ... for a special mission in the world", how many would say yes? "Manifest destiny"? The same.

Astonishingly, Taylor argues that stigmatizing certain other nations as evil can blind us to our own shortcomings, but there are in fact differences in the moral status of nations. Some are imperfect but striving to be better; some are evil and revel in being so. The world may now be starting to recognize that it may not be possible to be neutral, that one may have to choose. Can we simply tolerate Russia, Iran, North Korea?

5. Taylor recognizes that there are different points of view, but he recognizes only one as correct.

"While history is always told from a particular vantage point, if every American were able to receive a more accurate and honest baseline understanding of our nation's history, our conversations around who we are, what we value, and who we want to be would have common ground and be much less contentious."

6. Taylor says that our politics are corrupted today by identity politics, by seeing the other as evil, by attributing motives.

"Polarization—so often driven and exacerbated by distrust, anger, grievance, contempt, and vitriol—has poisoned our politics and public discourse. It has become one of the greatest threats to our democracy and civic health. ...[And, he claims to admire] deep commitment to disagree without impugning other participants' motives or character and to engage in ways that enable us to learn from and be changed by each other's perspectives, expertise, and convictions."

Yet, like a typical conspiracy theorist, he sees the motive of racial discrimination in virtually every Republican legislative action, Federal or state, in the last 50 years. Do you really think that the War on Drugs and the War on Crime were plots designed in order to incarcerate more Black males and weaken the Black community? Do you really think that voter fraud ended with Lyndon Johnson and Richard Daly (giving the presidency to JFK)? That we no longer need any election safeguards?

Attributing motive is a dangerous game.

For me, Taylor's book does not advance the discussion or shed light on the issues. It certainly fails to offer meaningful solutions.

Who Are We?

I have been waiting to wake from this nightmare before attempting to address the issues below, but I think I must acknowledge that, in fact, Donald Trump was President. However, I cannot reconcile that fact with my world view. So, after explaining my problem, I will continue by pretending it never happened. My problem is imagining how so many Americans could have voted for him. One could say it's just "those Republicans," but Trump is hardly a Republican and he twice got far more votes than there are party members. I know that elections are about choosing among the alternatives presented. In 2016, the alternative was understandably undesirable to many people. I certainly never would vote for her. But, I did. When the polls in Virginia tightened, I felt compelled to do my part to try to avoid Trump winning. But, in 2020, I do not believe many could have suspected Biden would be as bad as he has turned out to be. I refuse to believe that the motivation for most was racism. (Actually, I think Trump himself is not a racist, as such.) I do not think the primary motive was anti-immigration either; although, adverse views of how illegal immigration was being handled would be part of it. I suspect, but cannot prove, that profound unhappiness with our political leaders and with the smug elitism of the members of the establishment explains most of his votes. Sort of a protest or rebellion. The middle finger. But, it is unsettling that so many Americans could be so disillusioned as to vote for such a man. So, on to my subject.

We are a nation that emerged not from geography or ethnicity or conquest, but from choice. As observed by Francis Fukuyama, the United States is the successful example of a "creedal" nation, a nation based upon a commitment to a recognized creed, reflected in a set of foundational documents and principles. The idea is that people of different ethnicities, religions, family traditions and, perhaps, even languages can bond together to form a successful nation based upon common commitment to shared civic and political values. *The Origins of Political Order* (2011).

The founding settlors were quite diverse, representing very different religions, cultures and societal positions; although, most were from the United Kingdom and Western Europe, and most were Christian. The differences, however, were significant enough that wars had been fought over them in the Old World and that they were the source of significant conflict in the New. The colonies became a nation because they collectively chose to be one, and their people fought and died to do so. The new nation was established on a handful of documents declaring the basis of this new enterprise. The fundamental commitments were to individual liberty, private property, freedom of religion, separation of church and state, and equal justice and protection under the law, coupled with a deep distrust of government and of any concentrations of power.

The fact is that the United States is special and has been been a role model and an inspiration around the world. The United States has been a voice for human rights, a force against genocide, and a proponent of individual freedom, even if many of our efforts have been misguided or bungled. Founded on a set of unprecedented ideals and struggling to live up to them, we have set an example and established a standard. Our imperfect and unsuccessful efforts to live up to and realize fully those aspirations does not negate the standards but elevates them, makes them more human and more relevant.

"[T]he American founding couldn't be perfect from the start; it had to progress toward its goal. ...Prudence is the faculty that deals with imperfection in order to form, as the Preamble put it, a "more perfect union." **To make progress effectively and democratically, prudence seeks and finds necessary accommodations in compromise.** Not all compromises are successful, but the successful ones deserve to be accepted, and those who had the prudence to make them should be honored... ."

Harvey C. Mansfield,"The 'Systemic Racism' Dodge"
WSJ.com, September 18, 2020 (emphasis added).

Not everyone stayed to be part of the experiment at the end of the 19th century. (But, many, many others came willingly, even eagerly.) And, some had little choice—*e.g.*, slaves and indigenous peoples. After the Civil War, some former slaves left. most chose to stay. Subsequently, millions more came voluntarily to become part of this New World. Yet, a new nation created by and for diverse people accepting a common creed required land. Unfortunately, it came from (was taken from) the original occupants. However, when the colonists arrived, North America was a sparsely populated wilderness. The large, thriving civilizations that had existed in 1492 had been decimated and some even eliminated by the pandemics brought from the Old World.

The strength of the country came from the diversity and hard work of its inhabitants. The people were largely God-fearing and God-worshipping. Common characteristics were self-reliance, industriousness and neighborliness. There was an emphasis on being good citizens. Ironically, today, diversity refers to race, gender identification and sexual preference. I am referring to diversity of views, of ideas, of interests and abilities, of backgrounds, experiences and traditions, or economic circumstances.

Start with a question. Think of all the people you have encountered in life. Is the biggest or most important difference among them race? For me, the answer is an unambiguous "No". There are other differences that are profoundly more significant and much more relevant. Another question. Take a close look around you. Is the biggest, most important problem facing this country race (or White Privilege)? How about violence and lawlessness? Or, fraud and corruption? Or addiction (overdose deaths now exceeding 100,000 per year), or teen suicide (on the rise), or malnutrition, homelessness, severe poverty, child abuse, domestic abuse? Or Russian aggression, potential Chinese aggression, the threat of nuclear war. We face some serious challenges. Why single one out for so much attention?

The continuing surge in violence is quite troubling. So, is the rise in shoplifting and other crimes against individuals. But, I am most concerned by the apparent increase in theft from the government. Criminal tax evasion seems to be increasing—failure to report income and the hiding of assets. I am much more aware of Medicare and Medicaid fraud now. And of aggressive Ponzi schemes. (The reason may be that I receive a legal news report called *Law360 White Collar*, which chronicles new developments in white collar crime.) It is regularly surprising to me. We have had welfare and Social Security fraud for years, but that always seemed rather "small potatoes". But, the conduct involving the Covid relief programs set a whole new standard for anti-community behavior. Between abuse of the special unemployment payments and the PPP, we experienced the largest fraud in American history, with an estimated total stolen approaching $750 billion. While the populous cried out for more assistance in the crisis, thousands stole the benefits from those in need. Individual greed trumping community.

New 2022 plans for the IRS to become more aggressive are estimated to "yield more than $200 billion in revenue. ...The Joint Committee on Taxation, Congress's official tax scorekeeper, says that **from 78% to**

90% of the money raised from under-reported income would likely come from those making less than $200,000 a year. Only 4% to 9% would come from those making more than $500,000." The Editorial Board, "The IRS Is About to Go Beast Mode" *WSJ.com*, August 2, 2022 (emphasis added).

WHO WE WOULD BE

Is the goal of America to become "one people"? No. "One people" does not embrace diversity; it depends upon uniformity and conformity. *E Pluribus Unum* does not refer to the formation of "one people", but to the formation of one community, one nation, out of multiple peoples. The coming together of peoples for a cause, for a vision, for a nation.

There have been moments of true dignity in our history. Peggy Noonan describes one such:

> "The armies of the North and South, in blue and gray, were massed uneasily beyond the house. ... Some of Lee's officers had urged him not to surrender but to disband his army and let his men scatter to the hills and commence a guerrilla war. Lee had refused. ...Grant asked his aide Ely Parker, an American Indian of the Seneca tribe, to make a fair copy of the surrender agreement. When Lee ventured, 'I am glad to see one real American here.' Parker memorably replied, 'We are all Americans.'."
>
> "America's Most Tumultuous Holy Week," *WSJ.com*, April 14, 2022.

And, "..As he turned to leave, Grant came out to the steps and saluted him by raising his hat. Lee reciprocated and rode off slowly to break the news to the men he'd commanded." Lee's parting words to his troops: "'Leave the result to God. Go to your homes and resume your occupations. Obey the laws and become as **good citizens** as you were soldiers." *Id.* (emphasis added).

I previously tried to outline what constitutes being a good citizen. As I then noted, in the very early days of this country, George Washington wrote: "the Government of the United States gives to bigotry no sanction, to persecution no assistance, requires only that they who live under its protection should demean themselves as good citizens, in giving it on all occasions their effectual support."

The question for the future of this nation is what percentage of the population still believes in being a good citizen and in helping one's neighbors or, more importantly, is prepared to try to be a good citizen. The Greatest Generation is largely gone. My generation is fading. There are challenges facing our youth, including the decline in the roles of family, of the Church and of voluntary associations. Social life is increasingly online. That is a loss.

In person communities ask as well as give. Offering and accepting help are expanding and deepening experiences. Taking is a narrowing, inward experience. I worry that today's youth will not learn the meaning or experience the richness of community. Being good citizens? Do we still have the will? The shared vision? The courage? Do we even have the desire? Can we still strive to be people who "demean themselves as good citizens, in giving [this nation] on all occasions their effectual support"? Obey the law, pay your taxes, support our founding principles and be neighborly?

Mobility

I have had a special interest in issues of mobility for the last five years, but my attention was drawn to a different type of mobility when, in 2022, I read the 2010 book *The Price of Inequality* by Joseph E. Stiglitz. (Stiglitz is a Noble Prize winning economist who majored in Economics at Amherst College a decade before me. He was a legend in the Department.)

The issue is economic mobility in the United States. My interest was peaked because Stiglitz' assertions were so inconsistent with my own experience and my observations. He claims: "Belief in **America's essential fairness,** that we live in a land of equal opportunity, helps bind us together. That, at least, is **the American myth**, powerful and enduring. Increasingly, it **is just that—a myth**." *Id.*, p.17 (emphasis added).

I was surprised, so I looked at his sources. It turns out that the story is far more nuanced, more interesting and more informative than Stiglitz implies.

Stiglitz borrows this analogy from one of his sources:

"The **relationship between parents' income and that of their children is, in fact, very similar to that between parents' height and that of their children.** Alan Krueger... has pointed out, 'The chance of a person who was born to a family in the bottom 10 percent of the income distribution rising to the top 10 percent as an adult is about the same as the chance that a dad who is 5' 6" tall having a son who grows up to be over 6' 1" tall. It happens, but not often.'"'

Id., p.307 (emphasis added.

Think about it.

Height is determined by some combination of nature and nurture, of heredity, nutrition and life style. Over time, people have become significantly taller. The same is true of economic well-being. Family background matters because certain talents and abilities are genetically inherited, because certain skills are taught and because certain values and attitudes are transmitted by example. To isolate the impact of family income, we would need to control for genetic and family cultural inheritance. On average, tall offspring have tall parents. Is it not likely that, on average, people in the top quintile similarly will have more favorable genetic inheritances and more supportive families than those in the bottom quintile?

There are also several types of problems embedded in his analysis.

First, he brandishes a misleading yardstick, asserting that,

> "If America were really a land of opportunity, the life chances of success—of, say, winding up in the top 10 percent—of someone born to a poor or less-educated family would be the same as those of someone born to a rich, well-educated, and well-connected family. ...With full equality of opportunity, **20 percent of those in the bottom fifth would see their children in the bottom fifth.**"

Id., p.18 (emphasis added).

First, that conception of "equal opportunity" would be satisfied only by the completely random assignment of outcomes. Does anyone believe that everyone has (or should have) equal odds of achieving any particular outcome? That ability and effort play no role? Do we really think that family and background are (or should be) irrelevant? That would be quite shocking to people who take parenting seriously.

Second, his analogy suggests the next problem. What do we consider to be significant mobility? Does the offspring of the 5' 6" parents need to be 6' 1" to count as as evidence of height mobility or would 5' 10" be meaningful? Look at some of the examples of statistical mobility that Stiglitz considers insignificant :

- "...58 percent of children born to the bottom group make it out" *Id*. pp.18-19.
- "...8 percent of American men at the bottom rose to the top fifth." Jason DeParle, "Harder for Americans to Rise From Lower Rungs" *NYT.com*, January 4, 2012.
- "[A]bout 62 percent of Americans (male and female) raised in the top fifth of incomes stay in the top two-fifths..." *Id*.
- "...22 percent of Americans [raised in the bottom tenth of incomes stayed there as adults]." *Id*.
- "...26 percent of American men raised at the top tenth stayed there... ." *Id*.
- "About 36 percent of Americans raised in the middle fifth move up as adults, while 23 percent stay on the same rung and 41 percent move down... ." *Id*.

Do these numbers suggest lack of mobility to you? Did you, in believing the "myth", expect more?

Third, Stiglitz notes that there are studies indicating that the United States falls behind other developed countries in economic mobility. But, look at the studies. They acknowledge that the methodology used may prejudice the United States. The other countries have more compressed income scales, so a much smaller absolute income gain will move children into a higher income category. (This factor could partly explain why some analyses find less mobility where there is more unequality.) And, the analyses are intergenerational, requiring income data for both fathers and sons, thereby excluding many immigrants, who are particularly mobile in the United States. Also, the studies are based on fathers and sons, because that is the data available. Yet, women working is a very significant source of household mobility. *See, e.g.,* DeParle, "Harder for Americans to Rise From Lower Rungs"; Julia B. Isaacs, Isabel V. Sawhill, Ron Haskins, "Getting Ahead or Losing Ground: Economic Mobility in America", *The Brookings Institution*, February 2008. pp.37-45. Finally, these other countries tend to have more homogenous populations than the United States, making differences in family, upbringing and social environment less important determinants of outcome there than here.

Fourth, Stigitz central argument is founded on a misrepresentation of the "American dream". The promise is not that every person will succeed; it is that ability, hard work and determination will pay off. That you can be anything you want, not that you will. That dreams followed by appropriate actions can be realized, not just dreams standing alone. As Isaacs, Sawhill, Haskins explain (emphasis added): "Since our nation's founding, the promise of economic opportunity has been a central component of the American Dream. An economy that ... held out **the promise that hard work, vision, and risk—regardless of family background—would be rewarded.**"

"Perhaps the most remarkable byproduct of the growth of the American economy over the past century has been steady growth in the share of Americans who have been able to achieve a comfortable life and have every hope of seeing their children do even better. ...Americans strongly believe **that hard work and talent lead to economic success.** This underlying belief in the fluidity of class and economic status has differentiated Americans from citizens in the majority of other developed nations."

Id.

Finally, even Stiglitz' own sources conclude: "Even by measures of relative mobility, Middle America remains fluid. ...The 'stickiness' appears at the top and bottom, as affluent families transmit their advantages and poor families stay trapped." DeParle.

And, Isaacs, Sawhill, Haskins :

"We find considerable fluidity in American society. One's family background as a child, measured in terms of either income or wealth, has a relatively modest effect on one's subsequent success as an adult, especially if one grew up in middle-class circumstances. Those at the top or bottom of the ladder are somewhat less mobile."

Both statements contain probably the most important message for policy-makers. The poorest Americans are persistently the least mobile, at least on average. Of course, many of the most dramatic success stories came from the lowest economic rungs, but a large percentage of the poor stay poor. They seem trapped in a prison consisting of a toxic social environment, often coupled with neglectful or, even, abusive family circumstances. The children lack constructive examples and encouragement. The community in which they live cripples rather than empowers them. The trap of the poorest is the real problem the country faces concerning economic opportunities. It will not be solved by redistribution of wealth or income. Or, helped by talk about inequality. So, where are the insightful discussions of possible solutions?

Stiglitz predicts: "...[A]s the reality sinks in, as most Americans finally grasp that the economic game is stacked against them, all of this is at risk. Alienation has begun to replace motivation. Instead of social cohesion we have a new divisiveness." *Id.*, p.20.

Is that assertion really helpful? And, in fact, is it really right?

First, It appears that there are substantial numbers of Americans who still believe that hard work pays off. Recent survey data from *Echelon Insights* says: "Strong progressives don't evidence much faith in upper mobility, endorsing the ... statement on the questionable efficacy of hard work by 88-12. Hispanic voters, on the other hand, embrace the view that hard-working people are likely to get ahead by 55-39, as do working class voters by 55-40." Ruy Teixeira, "Working Class and Hispanic Voters Are Losing Interest ... : White College-Educated Voters ... Are On Board," *The Liberal Patriot,* July 14, 2022.

Second, it may be that Stiglitz has the causation reversed. Those who believe will make greater efforts, are more likely to notice even small successes and are much more likely to attribute their successes to their efforts. The disillusioned are likely not to try, not to recognize progress and to put good things down to chance. Of course, the believers are more likely to succeed and the disillusioned are much more likely to fail, those of both groups thereby proving to themselves that they were right.

Finally,

> "[In 2017,] [t]he average second-quintile household earned almost five times as much as the average household in the bottom quintile, because it had 2.4 times as many working-age members working and on average **each worker worked 80% more hours**. The average middle-quintile household earned almost 10 times as much and had 2.6 times the percentage of its working-age people working, each **working twice as many hours**. Yet **the bottom 60% of American households received essentially the same income after accounting for taxes, transfer payments and household size.**"

Phil Gramm and John Early, "Income Equality, Not Inequality, Is the Problem"
WSJ.com, August 29, 2022 (emphasis added).

There is the challenge to.the American Dream.

PHILOSOPHY and SCIENCE

Voice of the Unconscious

Reading about the planned release of two new books by Cormac McCarthy in the fall of 2022, I saw reference to his first nonfiction publication, which was in *Nautilus* in 2017, entitled "The Kekulé Problem: Where did language come from?" So I read it. It caused me to realize that in *Important Things,* I had not given enough attention to the nature and role of language or to the nature and role of the unconscious mind.

LANGUAGE

Undoubtedly one of the most significant and unique traits of human beings. I am referring to more than a shared association of a particular sound with a particular type of object, of a type of danger or a food, of a particular feeling. In such examples, sounds made are just a kind of body language addressed to the ears rather than the eyes, just as odors address the nose. All are forms of communication used by all animals. But, language? What distinguishes language?

Language does not require speech. It can be accomplished through signs or even signals. With language, words can convey abstract concepts and present narratives. Language can describe the past, the future, hopes and ideas. Perhaps most importantly, language enables exchanges, conversation, give and take.. Only humans tell stories, create narratives and converse.

So, "[r]eflective consciousness ... transforms communication into language... ." John Hands, *Cosmosapiens: Human Evolution from the Origin of the Universe* (2015), p.448. Language enables the transmission of information and ideas, of observations and speculation. As a result, it enables the collective accumulation of vast quantities of knowledge. Just visit any large library and look around. It also has aesthetic value in itself. Good writing does not just communicate ideas, but also feelings, emotions. The sound can be like music.

The origin or emergence of language is impossible to pinpoint or to investigate. Language leaves no footprints. It has no physical manifestation until the subsequent development of writing. We may find evidence of the physical faculties that could enable speech or of anatomical changes that might have arisen because greater facility to speak had adaptation value. But, that is it.

There is indirect evidence, however.

"It ... seems reasonable to hypothesize that painted or engraved symbols were paralleled by speech, however basic, that subsequently developed more sophistication. ...[P]articular achievements, like a group of humans migrating across 100 kilometres of ocean or trading in goods, require speech. Although the evidence of language in prehistoric times is necessarily indirect, it suggests that spoken language emerged in the Upper Palaeolithic."

Hands, *Cosmosapiens,* p.449.

Presumably, the appearance of language followed the development of some level of consciousness (for which we have no explanation, either) and after the beginnings of artistic expression. So, we can guess that it emerged about 50,000 years ago. One view is that language arose only once and then spread rapidly throughout human communities, because all known languages have similar structure. Perhaps, however, it appeared in several places, but maybe not entirely independently. There is no reason to think that it was the result of a genetic mutation or physical change. (There appears to be a relatively new gene—maybe about 100,000 years old—that seems to facilitate speech, which is a different matter.) Communication could well have developed from body language to sign language to speech. However, there must have been some predisposition existing in humans at the time. *

THE UNCONSCIOUS

Modern humans perceive that they think using language. We rehearse, debate, even fantasize using words in our heads, talking to ourselves. We even often have language as part of our dreams. Of course, we need our thoughts to be in language in order to communicate them. But, is that how they are formed?

We find it difficult to contemplate thinking without the use of language, but consider some commonplace occurrences. Have you ever said, "I can't find the words to express it"? Or, felt as if "a light went on" in your head when you suddenly understood something? What about solving problems in your sleep ("Let me sleep on it")? There are people who sleep with a notepad next to them to record ideas that come to them in their sleep. And, there are well-publicized claims of mathematical problems being solved while sleeping.

The title of McCarthy's article mentioned above is a reference to such an example, a dream of a snake with its tail in its mouth, forming a circle, causing the nineteenth century German scientist Friedrich August Kekulé to realize that the configuration of the benzene molecule is a ring. But, is this a case, as McCarthy argues, of the unconscious mind sending the answer in the form of an image or of the unconscious (or conscious) mind recognizing the answer in an image coincidentally appearing? The answer does not much matter for my purposes here. The point is that much of our "thinking" occurs without our awareness, that is, outside of our consciousness.

As to dreams, are they the mere rearrangement and disgorgement of the stuff stored in our subconscious, derived from our sensory facilities? Or, are they more, as Nick Bottom says in Act IV of Shakespeare's *Midsummer's Night Dream*:

> "I have had a most rare vision.
> I have had a dream
> past the wit of man
> to say what dream it was.
> Man is but an ass
> if he go about
> to expound this dream.
> ...
> The eye of man hath not heard,
> the ear of man hath not seen,
> man's hand is not able to taste, his
> tongue to conceive,
> nor his heart to report
> what my dream was."

(I thank my college classmate Dick Kellogg for bringing this soliloquy to my attention, in a totally different context.)

I have frequent dreams that are a jumble of recognizable images and excerpts of experienced events making little sense. But, I also have dreams of two types that are quite different. The first is a repeating creation of an imagined place and landscape, complete with an understanding of a map of the location so that I can find my way back on subsequent nights. In some, the central feature consists of a dramatic natural vista; in some, an interesting building, including the interiors; in some, a setting with buildings and natural features. In successive dreams, I will revisit and continue to explore these places until they return no more. The other odd type is the dream in which I make a lengthy presentation or speech. Occasionally, the setting returns a night or two later for me to continue. The contents of what I say are surprisingly coherent and often actually insightful. And, these dreams are not the reliving of past "glories." I could only wish. So, the one type of dream is mainly visual images, but in a realistic, logical and manipulatable arrangement, like a video game. The other type is essentially verbal, constructed mainly of words. And, they both reflect the input of imagination and of intelligence or logical thinking. How can that happen in the subconscious?

And, what about "near death" or "temporary death" experiences? The reports say that one's life "flashes before your eyes." Sometimes, one apparently observes and overhears what is going on around them.Maybe even sees one's own body. And, some survivors say that they find themselves in a new, unfamiliar place. How does this kind of thing happen? The wonder is not that it happens or, even, whether it happens, but that it is recognized and remembered. This interplay between the subconscious and consciousness is quite remarkable.

The cognitive process is apparently independent of language, and it largely occurs in our unconscious or subconscious mind. Now, I am not interested here in Freud's theory of repressed mental content. I use "unconscious" just in the sense of unaware and not intentional.

I am not talking about the more primitive part of the brain that operates our bodies, as here described:

"The **vertebrate** peripheral nervous system is divided into two. The **autonomic nervous system** comprises motor nerve fibres signalling to internal effector organs like the heart, lungs, and endocrine glands (which produce and secrete chemicals known as hormones into the blood circulation system to distant target cells where they regulate cellular metabolism) principally to maintain homeostasis, or regular functioning of the adult animal. It is regulated by the most ancient part of the central nervous system, the brain stem (which humans share with descendants of the earliest reptiles) responding automatically to stimuli. The **somatic nervous system** comprises motor nerve fibres signalling to effector organs, like muscles, principally on or near the outer layers of the animal; it is activated by the central nervous system responding to external, sensory stimuli and is under voluntary control."

Hands, *Cosmosapiens*, pp.400-401.

Humans, at least, appear to have additional, extremely important unconscious capabilities, including imagination, creativity and cognitive abilities like mathematics and problem solving. (Do these capacities exist in other mammals or in other life forms?) And, the unconscious "learns" with experience. We learn to ride a bike, to swim, to drive a car, to speak different languages. Some people even become superb musicians; others, world class athletes.

David Brooks quotes the neuropsychologist Elkhonon Goldberg as observing:

"Something rather intriguing has happened in my mind that did not happen in the past. Frequently, when I am faced with what would appear from the outside to be a challenging problem, the grinding mental computation is somehow circumvented, rendered, as if by magic, unnecessary. The solution comes effortlessly, seamlessly, seemingly by itself. What I have lost with age in my capacity for hard mental work, I seem to have gained in my capacity for instantaneous, almost unfairly easy insight."

The Second Mountain (2019), p.128.

And, what about prodigies? Just very fast learners?

According to a Noble prize winning physicist, "[p]sychophysics reveals that consciousness does not direct most actions, but instead processes reports of them, from unconscious units that do the work." Frank Wilczek. *Fundamentals : Ten Keys to Reality* (2021), p.xvii. "Humans themselves know many things that are not available to human consciousness, such as how to process visual information at incredible speeds, or how to make their bodies stay upright, walk, and run." *Id.*, p.205. And, from a contemporary Chinese science fiction writer: "the human brain was to some extent a problem-solving machine. ...Much of the process didn't require the participation of consciousness. Many important cognitive tasks were carried out subconsciously, with consciousness only providing supplemental functions like monitoring, storing, organizing, and refining." Baoshu, *The Redemption of Time* (2016), p.51.

How does the unconscious do these things? Not with words or through internal dialogue. That is how we organize, flesh out and make accessible the output of the thinking process. I rehearse the words before writing them. As Einstein reportedly said: "A new idea comes suddenly and in a rather intuitive way. That means it is not reached by conscious logical conclusions."

So, how do we think? How does it happen?

We just do not know.

In addition, we do not know how the unconscious knows the questions or how it communicates the answers to the conscious mind—neither how either one "speaks" nor how the other "hears." From my chair (wheelchair), I conclude that thinking must have preceded language, but how then did the unconscious and conscious mind operate without language?

The unconscious process is mysterious and extremely powerful. "By one calculation the mind can take in eleven million bits of information a second, of which the conscious mind is aware of forty. ... As Timothy Wilson of the University of Virginia put it, consciousness is like a snowball sitting on an iceberg. In other words, most of what guides us is not our conscious rationalization; it's our unconscious realm." Brooks, *The Second Mountain*, p.113.

It is clear that language opened vast opportunities for human social and intellectual interactions. But, is it also possible that the subsequent preeminence of language has imposed limitations on human beings by separating us from, or stifling, the voice of our unconscious? **

Is there a world we are missing because it is neither expressed nor, perhaps, expressible in language?

Because, "[m]any things are happening simultaneously within our brains, but our natural consciousness only allows us to attend to one at a time, and much is hidden from it altogether. As our ability to monitor and interpret brain state improve, it will be possible to present our inner selves to our perceiving self through our visual system, on displays, bypassing the filter of natural consciousness." Wilczek. *Fundamentals* , pp.185-6.

There are reasons to believe, and many hints to us, that the unconscious mind has potentials we can hardly imagine. ***

---

* Writing appeared only about 3,000-5,000 years ago, depending on what one considers to be writing. "Most linguistics scholars consider the earliest writing systems were cuneiform engraved on clay tablets from around 5,000 years ago in Sumer, Mesopotamia and Egyptian hieroglyphs engraved on stone from roughly the same period. ...Writing was invented independently in China, where the earliest evidence so far discovered consists of inscriptions on cattle shoulder-blades and tortoise shells used in divination rituals dating from around 1250 BCE in the Shang dynasty." Hands, *Cosmosapiens,* pp.449, 472.

** "What deadens us most to God's presence within us, I think, is the inner dialogue that we are continuously engaged in with ourselves, the endless chatter of human thought." Frederick Buechner, *Telling Secrets* (1991), p.105.

*** "The Greeks had a concept, later seized by Goethe, called the daemonic. A daemon is a calling, an obsession, a source of lasting and sometimes manic energy. Daemons are mysterious clusters of energy deep in the unconscious that were charged by some mysterious event in childhood that we imperfectly comprehend—or by some experience of trauma, or by some great love or joy or longing... ." Brooks, *The Second Mountain*, p.111.

Evil

A few months ago, I was asking myself this question: Have we outgrown evil? Then, in April 2022, I received this question from a friend from middle school in Northville, Michigan, who was reading the essays in *Wanderings of a Captive Mind*:

"A final thought or perhaps a question for you. Do you see Evil as part of your *Wanderings*?"

Of course.

But, what to say about it?

We have all seen evil.

Most recently, in the 90 minute long school shooting sprey in Ulvalde, Texas (and mass shootings around the country, some "hate crimes", some inexplicable). Before that, there was 9/11, Rwanda, ISIS, Sarajevo, the Khmer Rouge, on and on. Not just killings, but atrocities. The intentional infliction of terrible pain, of suffering, of terror. Premeditated and intentional. Poisonings, decapitations, violent rapes. Genocide.

We knew evil could still be perpetrated by rogue groups or by governments in secret. Indeed, sometimes evil seems to be just an inevitable part of the environment, like bad weather. But, now, we see evil from a civilized nation being executed out in the open, arrogantly, in a cloud of transparent lies. The assault on Ukraine is what should no longer happen. We had convinced ourselves that such acts were unthinkable in our new world. The events we are witnessing in the spring of 2022 must give rise to doubts in even the staunchest pacifist, the most dedicated advocate of nonviolence. Moral suasion did not stop the invasion of Ukraine; it is not deterring continuing widespread criminal behavior. (Perhaps, sometimes it becomes necessary for us to stand up to and oppose evil with our bodies, not just our words.)

Graeber and Wengrow assert that: "'Good' and 'evil' are purely human concepts ... made up in order to compare ourselves with one another." *The Dawn of Everything: A New History of Humanity* (2022), pp. 1-2. But, do we see either elsewhere in nature? As I wrote in *Important Things We Don't Know*, "we all know that evil exists, even if the idea offends our materialistic inclinations. Of course, it is a unique hallmark of *Homo sapiens*, if not of the genus *Homo*, at least on this world. It is curious that the concept exists in our minds; it is more curious that so much evil (violence, cruelty, greed, dishonesty, anger, vengefulness) appears among humans. How 'adaptive' is evil?"

There has also been a tendency to see evil as the result of institutions, social structures, philosophies or beliefs. But, sometimes we must realize that the evil is in the person.

> "All my life I had battled against an institutionalised evil. It had had a name and most often a country as well. ...But the evil that stood before me now was a wrecking infant in our own midst, and I became an infant in return, disarmed, speechless and betrayed. For a moment, it was as if my whole life had been fought against the wrong enemy. ...[T]**he evil was not in the system, but in the man.**"
>
> John le Carré, *The Secret Pilgrim*
> (1990), p. 377 (emphasis added).

As the sole Western survivor of the Cambodian terror camps says: Human beings: "The optimal being, the supreme creature, the natural aristocrat of the living world? Man who—when, exceptionally, he becomes his true self—can bring about excellence, but also bring about the worst. **A slayer of monsters, and forever a monster himself . . .**" Francois Bizot, *The Gate* (2002), p.6 (emphasis added).

A recent science fiction book is based, in part, on the premise that in the entire Universe, only humans engaged in deceIt: "deception was an important defensive weapon they had to consider, but to wield it, the Trisolarans first had to understand the only species known to possess such a capability—humans." Baoshu, *The Redemption of Time*, p.36.

We all probably remember knowing children who seemed possessed, driven to misbehave, to act up or act out. Such children tend to grow up and find ways to manage their demons. Adults, of course, regularly commit bad acts, but in most of these people, there exists a core of vulnerability, of humanity, with some capacity for empathy. The worst people are self-centered, calculating, manipulating and greedy. But, even most of these people still have a human core. Most, not all. There are some sociopaths. These people never ask forgiveness, never apologize. They embrace their actions. They do not blame their behavior on temptation or on others, except in order to manipulate someone. They are certainly cynical, they certainly do harm, but are they "evil"?

I have no answer. I have only known two probable sociopaths in my life, to one of whom I was married for over 40 years.

MORAL JUDGMENT

Yet, the point of this essay is closer to home. It is about the desirability of reincorporating moral judgment into our society, our relationships and our lives.

In our relativistic modern world, good and evil were seeming increasingly anachronistic. We could make no quality distinctions among cultures, religions, traditions or personal proclivities. Everything was relative. A continuum, colored by our prejudices, of course, but still a continuum. For example, as an adult, I have struggled to consider the behavior resulting from mental illness as just symptoms of disease, despite the hurt being done to others, often to innocent people. Indeed, with respect to many aspects of personality or traits, we do all fall somewhere along a continuum.

(Yet, those people who oppose—or favor—abortion, who are homophobic, who are racist or sexist, or who are libertarians are ... what? Misguided or lost?)

So, do we still value character? Is it even relevant any more? Perhaps, we have "outgrown" the need for responsible adults. We have government, schools, universities and other institutions to protect us and take care of us, to shelter us and to comfort us when the sheltering is insufficient. A little whining can go a long way. And, medication: Pharmaceutical solutions to our problems. And, drugs for distraction.

A mandatory instruction for late twentieth century parents was "it is always the act that is bad, never the child." Well, okay. But, that approach can be misunderstood by children. It can separate acts from responsibility.

We may continue to wonder, by the way, are there bad people or only bad acts?

RESPONSIBILITY

The problem today is that "[w]e ... are morally inarticulate. We're not more selfish or venal than people in other times, but we've lost the understanding of how character is built." David Brooks, *The Road to Character* (2015), p.5. Where we draw a line between normal and abnormal (illness) is pretty arbitrary. "[W]e have obscured the inescapable moral core of life with shallow language ... and thus become increasingly blind to the moral stakes of everyday life." *Id.*, p.54.

In my precollege days, I did not recognize mental "illness". Harmful aberrant behavior was simply bad. Lying, manipulating or using others, abusiveness, all were wrong, inside a family or out.

We all have our own personal demons (for me, a violent temper, a tendency toward self-righteousness and reoccurring bouts of self-centeredness). But, I was taught that these were the things against which I was expected to fight, to struggle—a bit like a Whac-A-Mole game. The goal was to overcome them, recognizing that that goal can never be fully achieved. Small steps. Progress today. Success. Then, ...

The successes and failures experienced during our daily challenges to be better are what develop character. Despite the contrary advice of modern psychiatrists, psychologists, child rearing experts and life coaches, I think we need to try to own our weaknesses and faults, to struggle with ourselves, to confront our demons and to recognize that life is not just about "me".

The development of character is part of the transformation of a child into a responsible, contributing adult, into someone who can and will protect his or her family and community. Something my generation saw in Westerns like *Bonanza*, *The Man Who Shot Liberty Valance* and *The Magnificent Seven*.

There is something quite compelling about Catholic confession. "Father, forgive me for I have sinned." An admission that one has done wrong. Powerful. And, made with confidence in a forthcoming forgiveness. Yes. So much more to the point than the long-winded and mushy Presbyterian statements of confession that I hear on Sundays. "I have sinned" acknowledges that I did something. Not that it just happened or happened to me, but that it was a volitional act, one for which I ask forgiveness. That is owning one's own actions.

WHY BOTHER?

Yet, one might ask, why?

Why grow up? Why not all aspire to live like Peter Pan?

Well, I guess the answer is "for ourselves".

The meaningful, satisfying experiences in life involve struggle, sacrifice and loss. They involve confronting ourselves. They are moral events. Things are not, or should not be, just different shades of gray.

We need especially to judge ourselves. To expect and to demand personal responsibility and personal accountability, from ourselves as well as from others.

As John Steinbeck wrote in *East of Eden*:

"Humans are caught—in their lives, in their thoughts, in their hungers and ambitions, in their avarice and cruelty, and in their kindness and generosity too—in a net of good and evil. I think **this is the only story we have** and that it occurs on all levels of feeling and intelligence. **Virtue and vice were warp and woof of our first consciousness**, and they will be the fabric of our last....**A man, after he has brushed off the dust and chips of his life, will have left only the hard clean questions: Was it good or was it evil? Have I done well—or ill?**"

Quoted in Brooks, *The Second Mountain*
(2019), p. 47 (emphasis added).

SIN

And, sin?

David Brooks put the matter as follows:

"Sin is a necessary piece of our mental furniture because it reminds us that **life is a moral affair.** No matter how hard we try to reduce everything to deterministic brain chemistry, no matter how hard we try to reduce behavior to the sort of herd instinct that is captured in big data, no matter how hard we strive to replace sin with nonmoral words, like 'mistake' or 'error' or 'weakness,' **the most essential parts of life are matters of individual responsibility and moral choice: whether to be brave or cowardly, honest or deceitful, compassionate or callous, faithful or disloyal.**"

So, we need more sin, but less evil?

Actually, I have trouble with Brooks' use of sin. A prominent theme inthis book is that mankind is fundamentally flawed (original sin), which he refers to as the "crooked timber" viewport (after Immanuel Kant: "Out of the crooked timber of humanity, no straight thing was ever made") and the essential role of grace or unconditional love. I may not fully understand his argument, but I think most of what Brooks says can stand powerfully without this biblical overlay. Brooks also contrasts "moral realism" with "moral relativism", using philosophical schools of thought to explain his position, but I think that this context is as unnecessary as the religious one.

I perceive mankind as born with a moral capacity—maybe even a moral compass—but certainly a moral craving. At the same time, we are physically mammals, with the drives and needs of all mammals— for food, shelter and reproduction. We also seem to have some rather unique inclinations like greed, envy and pride. And, we clearly have weaknesses. But, our mammalian instincts push us to take the safe road, the easy path. We are inclined to sit rather than stand, to duck rather than stand up, to evade rather than embrace responsibility. This is where upbringing, life examples and expectations come in.

Yet, as suggested, I have trouble with "original sin". I am more com-fortable with the view of the new born as an innocent with the potential for sin and also for rising above. It is the things that happen as the child grows that have moral dimensions. The decisions and the choices and the actions. Those can be morally good or bad. As Brooks says in the passage quoted above: "whether to be brave or cowardly, honest or deceitful, compassionate or callous, faithful or disloyal" Whether one strives to be better, to do the right thing. Whether one sees the moral fabric of life, of living, of the inevitable forks in the road.

"Once the necessities for survival are satisfied, **the struggle against sin and for virtue is the central drama of life**. ...You become more disciplined, considerate, and loving through a thousand small acts of self-control, sharing, service, friendship, and refined enjoyment. ...Each struggle leaves a residue. A person who has gone through these struggles seems more substantial and deep. ...There's joy in a life filled with interdependence with others, in a life filled with gratitude, reverence, and admiration. **There's joy in freely chosen obedience to people, ideas, and commitments greater than oneself**."

Brooks, *The Road to Character*,
pp.263, 264, 268, 269 (emphasis added).

For a less traditional perspective on original sin, I turn to a twentieth-century Jesuit priest and scientist:

"As far as the mind can reach, looking backwards, we find the world dominated by physical evil, impregnated with moral evil (sin is manifestly 'in potency' close to actuality as soon as the least spontaneity appears)—we find it in a state of original sin. ... **[Perhaps]** ... **original sin expresses, translates, personifies, in an instantaneous and localized act, the perennial and universal law of imperfection which operates in mankind in virtue of its being '*in fieri*'** [in the **process of becoming**]."

Pierre Teilhard de Chardin,
Christianity and Evolution: Reflections on Science and Religion
(1969), pp.47, 51 (emphasis added).*

SO?

I agree that we need to reintroduce "sin" into our vocabulary and into our view of the world. We need to recognize, acknowledge and name the bad, the disappointing, the demeaning and dehumanizing. If we learn to make moral judgments and distinctions again, to acknowledge sin; we might regain the strength, and fashion new tools, to confront evil.

Maybe, then...

More sin,
Less evil.

---

* "One might even, perhaps, go so far as to say that since the creative act (by definition) causes being to rise up to God from the confines of nothingness (that is, from the depth of the multiple, which means from some other matter), all creation brings with it, as its accompanying risk and shadow, some fault.... . Seen in this way, the drama of Eden would be the very drama of the whole of human history concentrated in a symbol profoundly expressive of reality." *Id.*, pp.51-52.

Contradiction

I owe this essay to my daughter. She took a multi disciplinary course during her year at Amherst College called Eros and Insight. She has talked about it ever since. The topic was "sustaining contradiction" in living. It has taken me several years and some new challenges for me to begin to grasp the power and role of the contradictions, of opposites, of the irreconcilable in the human experience. As she says:

> "To me that is the Absurd.
> The sustaining of contradiction.
> The uncomfortable truth."

Man is uniquely "blessed" with conciousness and reason, but he lives in an unreasonable world. That is the fundamental contradiction. And, it has been much discussed.

Look at the following three composite quotations:

> "[W]e live in the contradiction between these two ... . The outer, majestic ... and the inner, humble ... are not fully reconcilable. We are forever caught in self-confrontation. We are called to fulfill both personae, and must master the art of living forever within the tension between these two natures. ...By successfully confronting sin and weakness we have the chance to play our role in a great moral drama. We can shoot for something higher than happiness."

David Brooks, *The Road to Character* (2015).

"Man stands face to face with the irrational. He feels within him his longing for happiness and for reason. The absurd is born of this confrontation between the human need and the unreasonable silence of the world. ...From the moment absurdity is recognized, it becomes a passion, the most harrowing of all. ...I can understand only in human terms. What I touch, what resists me—that is what I understand. And these two certainties—my appetite for the absolute and for unity and the impossibility of reducing this world to a rational and reasonable principle—I also know that I cannot reconcile them."

Albert Camus, *The Myth of Sisyphus and Other Essays* (1942).

"In thinking about our own existence, we are often struck by two contrary thoughts. One is that nothing could be more accidental. It is depressingly easy to imagine the world without me. The other is that my nonexistence is absolutely inconceivable. The world needs me to be complete. ...The knowledge of death and the idea of eternity are the two sides of a single coin. They are born together and together make us human. ...What the idea of eternity does do is allow us to form ambitions and engage in pursuits, personal and collective, that cannot be brought to completion in any span of time, ...to set goals that are not confined by time, though we ourselves are. ...Pursuits of this uniquely human kind, with their mix of disappointment and joy, are what remain of the idea of eternity and our desire to reach it once the confidence that we can is gone. ...Yet we not only accept the paradox. We live by it."

Anthony T. Kronman, *After Disbelief: On Disenchantment, Disappointment, Eternity, and Joy* (2022).

OPPOSITES

Opposites play an important part in our conceptualization of our world. Black and white, up and down, good and evil, alive and dead, short and tall, and so on. They are part of the way we think, the way we communicate. Through contrasts. One versus another. Humans categorize and compare to make sense of the world. As noted above and below, our sense of the eternal derives from our awareness of our mortality.

But, what I write about here are the circumstances in which we embrace opposites, times when we must accept and sustain contradiction. Does that sound like nonsense?

"A basic duality in human nature has been evident from the emergence of humans, manifested in such things as cooperation versus competition, selflessness versus selfishness, and compassion versus aggression. It has been seen as a conflict between good and evil... ." John Hands, *Cosmosapiens: Human Evolution from the Origin of the Universe*, p.558. But, I am referring here to the impact of the essential unity of that duality on human experience. Our consciousness leads to our awareness of our own deaths, which gives us the awareness of time and eternity. Consciousness creates the fundamental contradiction of human existence.

David Hume expressly distinguished between "relations of ideas"and "matters of fact", the former including mathematics and logic, subject to deductive reasoning with the consequent necessity of the conclusions because contrary conclusions would be logically contradictory. In contrast, "The contrary of every matter of fact is still possible; because it never implies a [logical] contradiction... . **Were it demonstratively false, it would imply a contradiction, and could never be distinctly conceived by the mind.**" *An Enquiry concerning Human Understanding and Other Writings* (2007) (edited by Stephen Buckle), pp.28–29,

36 (originally published in 1748 and entitled *Philosophical Essays concerning Human Understanding*) (emphasis added).

Logic says that two propositions that contradict each other cannot both be true, so the demonstration that a statement logically leads to a contradiction constitutes a "proof" that the statement is not true. Clearly, this conception seems to be integral to the notion of rational thought and logic. Following Immanuel Kant, Hadley Arkes states that "[t]he law of contradiction expresses a necessary truth, and all efforts to refute it will fall into **the embarrassment** of self-contradiction." *First Things: An Inquiry into the First Principles of Morals and Justice (1986).*, p.51 (emphasis added).

In that philosophical tradition, Arkes identifies "necessary truths" as thngs that can be known independent of experience (*a priori* facts that must be so). They are innate to the human cognitive process. These "truths" include space, time, causality and "the law of contradiction". *Id.*, pp.51–84. But, are these concepts actually empirical, that is, do they reflect facts, things that are true (or untrue) about the physical world? A "necessary truth" may be "necessary" in terms of the functioning of the human mind, but is it necessarily "true"?

It may be that we are incapable of rationally conceiving of two contradictory propositions both being true, but our reason does not control or determine the actual relationships of the world, as twentieth century science has shown. I have already written at length about logic, mathematics and quantum mechanics and the contradictions that arise: Heisenberg's uncertainty principle; Gödel's incompleteness theorems; Schrödinger's cat; things that are both particles and waves; things that are both here and there (and, perhaps, everywhere); indeterminacy until observation; instantaneous travel.

THE ABSURD: THE VITAL TENSION

There is more in, and to, life than logic and facts.

Above, I present three composite quotations from writings 80 years apart. They speak about contradiction and paradox being at the heart of the human experience, as being the key to what it is to be human. Camus took atheism as a given or the starting point and articulated a philosophy of the absurd (Existentialism)—The Absurd Man. Kronman claims to have started as an Existentialist, following his mother (and Camus), but through the confrontation with contradiction, finds faith in the Divine. Brooks says he undertook his exploration "to save his soul."

The element of contradiction is certainly central to Christianity: Found in the Cross, in Christ's entrance into Jerusalem celebrated on Palm Sunday (a King mounted on a donkey), in the Beatitudes, in the belief that one must lose his life in order to find it ("For whosoever will save his life shall lose it: and whosoever will lose his life for my sake shall find it." *Matthew* 16:25-26, King James Version.) It is also present in the Old Testament (as in the Book of Job and the prophet Isaiah).

"Lord, I believe—help Thou mine unbelief."
(*Mark* 9:24)

David Brooks writes of a Puritan prayer he finds called "The Valley of Vision" (*The Second Mountain*, p.232):

"The first line is 'Lord, high and holy, meek and lowly.'...The rest of the text summarizes the whole inverse logic of faith: The broken heart is the healed heart. The contrite spirit is the rejoicing spirit. The repenting soul is the victorious soul. Life in my death. Joy in my sorrow. Grace in my sin. Riches in my poverty. Glory in my valley."

Similarly,

> "It was the vital growth of this faith, even when he was too much troubled to recognize the fact, that made him **strong in the midst of weakness**; when the son of man in him cried out, 'Let this cup pass', the son of God in him could yet cry, 'Let thy will be done'. **He could 'inhabit trembling,' and yet be brave.**"

George McDonald. *Thomas Wingfold, Curate* (emphasis added).

Embracing contradiction is the essence of faith. And, *vice versa*. And, the source of the richness of human life; the key to appreciation of life and of all of its wonders. Humor in tragedy; tears in comedy; knowledge in ignorance; strength in weakness; insight in farce; defiance in surrender. And, most of all, hope, despite ... .

I have always been obsessed with the bittersweet, with the experience of bitter and sweet together, simultaneously. Bittersweet experiences, bittersweet novels, bittersweet movies and bittersweet music (*Hallelujah, Danny Boy, O Holy Night*, much of country music). And, of course, dark chocolate, rhubarb pie, cranberries, sour apples. The things that give life depth and breadth.

Our consciousness and reason lead to contradictions, and we feel ... what?

Embarrassment?

No. Not at all.
More like awe and wonder.

Time, Eternity and Us

I have written several dozens of pages on the meaning and nature of time, but I still feel something is missing.

So, I offer some more thoughts on Time, Eternity and Us.

TIMELESS

Start with what we mean by eternal. It can be used to refer to endless time, time without end. It is also used to refer to timelessness, somehow outside of time. Modern cosmology assures us that the Universe is not eternal, that it will have an end. Some physicists conclude, therefore, that time must also have an end. However, if time has an end, then it almost certainly has a beginning. (The arguable consistency between that conclusion and certain religious beliefs bothers some scientists, but that is a different matter.) So, if time is not endless, can anything be timeless, or is that just an expression we use, like "timeless beauty"?

Well, we often talk about mathematics as being timeless, as being always true and unchanging (*i.e.*, eternal). Arguably, the same could be said about logic more generally and, indeed, about theoretical science. What we mean is that mathematics is not dependent upon time, it is not affected by time, it is not temporal. We can say it exists outside of time. Likewise, science is based on the premise that there exist Laws of Nature that are eternal in both senses of the word—everlasting and independent or outside of time. We may only know approximations of those Laws, but we believe they exist and that we can come closer and closer to discovering them. That is what science is about.

When we examine, discuss or even think about time, we effectively step outside of time and make it an object. In addition, we imagine eternity. We routinely contemplate the future. And, the past. We exercise our imagination in all sorts of ways. None of these things are time dependent, like causal relationships (the cause necessarily preceding the effect in time). Of course, we do all of these things "in time", but that is a different concept.

Other examples of timelessness can be found even in the physical world, according to theoretical physics. Einstein's General Theory characterizes the physical world as existing in four dimensional space-time in which travel in the four dimensions is subject to a universal speed limit, generally assumed to be the speed of light. Thus, when light is traveling through three dimensional space (at the speed of light, naturally), it can not be traveling through time, *i.e.*, it is necessarily timeless. It does not age; it is eternal. The same would be true for any and all things that are traveling at the speed of light!. But, you might say, it takes light 8 minutes to travel to the Earth from the moon, so isn't that light 8 minutes older? No, it has not aged. It is the very same light that originated earlier, just being observed later.

(Similarly, an object that is completely motionless in three dimensional space will be traveling only through time. This implication is somewhat ambiguous given the assumption in Einstein's Special Theory that there is no absolute space.)

Indeed, the one-way flow of time is simply not part of most of modern physics. Perhaps, the passage of time simply is not part of physical reality. We experience it profoundly, but that may be a purely human phenomenon. The passage of time may be an integral part of how we think and perceive the world, but perhaps it is not part of the world outside of us.

So, timelessness is not such a rare characteristic after all. Furthermore, physicists tell us that the elemental particles, as well as many types of atoms, will exist unchanging forever. Thus, it is said that the stuff of our bodies comes from the stars and will return to the stars. Matter and energy, it seems, are eternal.

ETERNAL

But, "the eternal" is still an essentially human phenomenon; it exists because we exist.

Some physical aspects of eternity may be present, but it is only through human awareness that is it realized. Just like time itself. Color and sound may exist without us, because animals can see and hear. But, not eternity. It is only human beings with our unique awareness of, and anticipation of, death that perceive timelessness. We bring the eternal into the world.

> "The knowledge of death is the awareness of a time longer than the period allotted to me: of a time 'before' and 'after' my life.... The power that allows me to conceive a time longer than my life throws the brevity of my existence into painful relief. ...It allows us to consider the world and ourselves from **a vantage point other animals can never attain.** ...[T]he uncanny power to see that we are living in time, as opposed to merely doing so ... ."

Anthony T. Kronman, *After Disbelief: On Disenchantment, Disappointment, Eternity, and Joy* (2022), pp.30, 32 (emphasis added). *

If we are what brings the eternal into our world, what else does our existence do? Is there something more we can say about our role?

HUMAN

I have written elsewhere about the nature of Consciousness, the Anthropic Principle, the Fine-tuning Problem and our (human's) Role in the Universe. I have previously noted how humans (as conscious, self-reflective entities) introduced awe, joy and beauty into the Universe; that a star might have always emitted electromagnetic waves, but only with the presence of we humans does it "shine" and "twinkle".

I want to take those speculations a step further.

There is the quantum mechanics view:

> "The distinguished theoretical physicist John Wheeler... took the conscious-dependent view of physical reality to its logical conclusion. He argued that the universe depends for its existence on the presence of conscious observers to make it real, not only today but also retrospectively to the Big Bang. The universe existed in a kind of indeterminate probabilistic ghost state until conscious beings observed it, thus collapsing the wave function for the entire universe and bringing it into physical existence."

John Hands, *Cosmosapiens: Human Evolution from the Origin of the Universe* (2016), pp. 87-8.

But, I am thinking of something different, although possibly related.

Take the question: "Why is there something rather than nothing?" One answer is: "Because we exist." The reason that is an answer to the question is that if we did not exist, then the question would never be asked. Now, this example seems a bit gimmicky. Like a word game.

Take another example.

We can assert that since we exist, the Universe has to be the way it is (because if it were not, we would not).

We might also plausibly assert that because we exist, the Universe is as it is.

This last formulation carries a different implication. It suggests causation. Not causality as we normally understand it, with its mandatory temporal implications; but, causality pursuant to what is called a "teleological" explanation. The goal or function to be achieved causes the circumstances necessary to its realization. Somehow, it pulls along everything else in order to make the appearance of the desired result, not only possible, but actual.

Or, alternatively, there are tendencies toward certain end results that influence how things are, moving the world towards those ends. Indeed, visions of the future shape the here-and-now. The preexisting function or goal is the reason the Universe is as it is. Because we humans with consciousness exist, the Universe must be as it is and, also, is why it is as it is. In order for us to be here, the Universe was created; it was created for that purpose.

Is this argument subject to the same characterization as the prior example—rather gimmicky?

Not for me.

MAYBE

The status of teleological explanations—that things happen for (because of) a reason or objective— is hotly debated. For obvious reasons, it is rejected, even loathed, by most scientists, but the views of philosophers are more mixed. The problem is the suggestion of intention. This type of explanation works well for human creations—the object is as it is because that is what its creator wanted, it is that way because of the function it was intended to perform, its function is why it looks as it does or is as it is. However, intention is not a necessary part of teleology.

There is certainly evidence of the acceptance, and even the embrace, of such explanations by earlier civilizations. Indeed, teleology is at the heart of Aristotle's metaphysics. It also appears in the works of Kant, Hegel and Marx. And, "there is disagreement as to whether or not Darwin's evolutionary explanations are teleological. Even Darwin's contemporaries disagreed ... ."

> "In any case, it is clear that Darwin used the language of 'final causes' to describe the function of biological parts in his Species Notebooks and throughout his life; he also reflected frequently about the relationship between natural selection and teleology."

> Colin Allen and Neal Jacob, "Teleological Notions in Biology", *The Stanford Encyclopedia of Philosophy* (Spring 2020 Edition).

Or, perhaps, self-reflective consciousness was somehow built into the fabric of the Universe at the beginning, as a part of the creation itself, so we are an inevitable part of evolution. "[O]nce it has emerged from the inorganic, life continues naturally, and in a combined two-fold movement, to become both [more complex] externally and more conscious internally; and this extends up to the psychological emergence of reflection." Pierre Teilhard de Chardin, *Christianity and Evolution: Reflections on Science and Religion,* p.230.

The real question is not whether we find such explanations to be illuminating, but whether they actually capture any part of reality. But, to find evidence of that, we must have our eyes open, open to the possibility.

We need to be willing to expand our minds.

---

* I wrote this essay shortly after reading *After Disbelief:* I have borrowed the starting point, the two meanings of eternal. There are also a few similarities in what follows, but I do not find many of his arguments nor his conclusions to be persuasive, and I end in a different place.